Mountain Painter

MOUNTAIN PAINTER
An Autobiography
by W Heaton Cooper

Dedicated to Ronald Mann, who
first thought that I should write this book.

Acknowledgments

I would like to express my deep gratitude to the 39 owners of my paintings who have kindly allowed photographs to be taken of them.

Also to the following for their assistance:

Border Television for the last illustration.

Burrswood Home of Healing, Kent – photograph.

Mrs Betty Cameron – photograph.

Sidney Cross O.B.E. – loan of crag drawings.

Fell and Rock Climbing Club – use of crag drawings.

Guest, Keen and Nettlefolds Ltd – photograph.

Bob Klose – for taking excellent colour photographs.

Mrs Ruth Hargreaves – loan of drawing.

David Howell – loan of colour slide.

Ronald Mann – for reading M.S. and making helpful suggestions.

The late Athol Murray – photograph.

Leslie Sparey – use of three colour slides.

Studio magazine – use of colour plate.

United Kingdon Atomic Energy Authority – photograph.

Colin Baker, Managing Director, Frank Peters Ltd. – for publishing this book.

Ronnie Mullin, Designer – for putting it together so well.

Also to my four children for reading M.S. and making helpful suggestions.

SCAFELL PIKE FROM
UPPER ESKDALE (1936)

All day I had been climbing with two friends on Scafell. A thunderstorm had been slowly brewing throughout the afternoon and, as we made our way hurriedly down from Mickledore and across the head of the valley, clouds began to loiter around the peaks, smoky grey against a murky yellow sky.

As we were stepping out on the slopes of Yeastyriggs Crag I looked back. It was like a Chinese painting come to life. Simple colour, from the straw-coloured sky into which the higher peaks melted, down through deepening shades of violet-blue, among them the thin gold thread of a stream catching the light, culminating in the dark indigo double-mass of Esk Buttress.

I had only a sketchbook with me so I drew a few lines to remind me of the design and ran to catch up the others.

The scene haunted me for several weeks until I took a piece of paper, flooded it very wet with cadmium yellow, quickly adding the paler wreaths of cloud in cobalt blue and vermilion while the paper was still wet, the more dark and definite slopes of cloud added in dry blue-violet paint before the original wash had time to dry, and, with dry colour laid in the lower darker slopes, adding light red to the purples until the foreground slopes were painted with a touch of burnt sienna to bring them nearer. All this first stage of the painting had to be done very rapidly before the first wash had time to dry, taking about five or six minutes.

When the paper was quite dry I put in the dark Esk Buttress, the point of immediate interest and, to me, importance of the picture, painting it in cobalt blue and vermilion, with a touch of crimson, so that it was the bluest object in the painting, in contrast to the upward yellowing of the tones, culminating in the sky. The foreground rocks were painted in ultramarine – a nearer colour than cobalt – and burnt and raw sienna in the lighter passages.

We raced across the face of Bowfell and down the Band, arriving to a warm welcome at the Old Dungeon Ghyll Hotel, Langdale just as the storm broke.

Contents

List of Illustrations xii
Introduction xiv
Chapter
1 Forebears 1
2 Parents 7
3 Childhood 13
4 Youth 19
5 Sussex 27
6 Loss 35
7 Climbs 41
8 Decision 51
9 Marriage 61
10 Home 71
11 Painting Mountains 77
12 Winterseeds 85
13 Commissions 95
14 Scotland 103
15 Europe 111
16 Conference 117
17 Ophelia 123
18 Onwards 129
19 Hope 139

List of Illustrations

1   Scafell Pike from Upper Eskdale (1934)   vii
2   Mischabel Range from Triffthorn, Swiss Alps (1965)   xiv
3   Sheep Dipping at Nibthwaite (1968)   xxii
4   Ballholm and Ese Fjord, Norway (1966)   1
5   My Father (1907)   2
6   Fjaerlands Ford, Norway (1966)   2
7   Levers Water above Coniston (1960)   5
8   My Mother, Ellide, Frithjof and Myself (1908)   7
9   My Family at our home at Balholm (1907)   7
10 Autumn Flames, Norway (1968)   8
11 February Snows in Little Langdale (1983)   11
12 Frithjof (1926)   13
13 Fairyland of Snow, Rydal (A. Heaton Cooper, 1927)   13
14 Blencathra from Guard House (1971)   14
15 Codale Tarn (A. Heaton Cooper, 1927)   15
16 Climbers in Easter Gully, Dow Crag (1924)   17
17 Rapids on the Esk (1956)   19
18 East Buttress, Scafell (1936)   20
19 Kern Knotts Chimney, Gable (1934)   21
20 Scafell from Mickledore (1935)   21
21 Evening, Thirlmere (1964)   22
22 Reflections, Thirlmere (1936)   25
23 Eagles Nest, Gable (1937)   27
24 Les Calanques, Provence (1925)   28
25 Grey Crags, Buttermere (1936)   29
26 The Sanctuary Garden (1925)   29
27 Upper Eskdale (1971)   30
28 The Rocky Shore of Wastwater (1972)   33
29 Tophet Bastion, Gable (1937)   35
30 Boat People, Buenos Aires (1931)   36
31 Fairfield Range from Graithwaite (1952)   37
32 Langstrath Beck (1962)   38
33 Aconcagua, Argentina (1931)   41
34 Rio Mendoza, Argentina (1931)   42
35 Foot of Gimmer Crag, Langdale (1933)   43
36 Evening, Pillar (1934)   44
37 Y Garn from Tryfan, Wales (1937)   45
38 Jim Cameron (1979)   46
39 Scafell from Beckhead, Winter (1934)   47
40 Blea Tarn, November (1982)   49
41 In a Film Studio (1936)   51
42 Harry Kelly (1937)   52
43 Kelly on North Wall, Pillar (1937)   52
44 Scafell Crag (1936)   53
45 With A. B. Hargreaves on Pillar (1937)   54
46 Gordon and Craig Route, Dow Crag (1936)   54
47 The Silent Quarry, Little Langdale (1954)   55
48 On Sty Head (1936)   55
49 Building the Studio, Grasmere (1938)   56
50 Rydal Oak (1955)   57
51 Hazy Morning, Crummock Water (1956)   59
52 The Shadowed Farm, Troutbeck (1964)   61
53 Anthony Chapman, Huntsman (1967)   62
54 Shamrock, Pillar (1935)   63
55 The Road to Crummock Water (1952)   63
56 Dawn over the Scafells (1981)   64
57 Ennerdale in Spring (1980)   65
58 Family Carols (1950)   65
59 Buttermere Village (1969)   66
60 Shepherd and Lamb (1964)   66
61 Tarn on Blake Rigg (1972)   67
62 Spring, Head of Buttermere (1982)   69
63 Bernard Eyre-Walker (by Tom Dearden 1972)   71
64 Upstream in Rannerdale (1979)   72
65 Morning in Early Spring, Grasmere (1969)   73
66 Langdale Pikes from Lingmoor (1938)   75
67 Design for Plate 66   77
68 First Stage   77

69	Near Same Subject in November (1940)	77
70	Sketch for Windermere from Red Screes (1981)	78
71	The Island, Grasmere (1973)	79
72	Dawn Light on Mont Blanc (1956)	80
73	Matterhorn from Gornergrat (1956)	80
74	Grasmere from Helm Crag (1963)	83
75	Wetherlam from Langdale Fell (1973)	85
76	Winterseeds Welcome (1950)	86
77	Ophelia, Heaton, Julian and Clare (1954)	86
78	Weisshorn from Gornergrat (1955)	87
79	Steel Fell Tarn (1962)	88
80	Blaven, Skye (1982)	89
81	The Osmastons (1983)	89
82	Young Wordsworth (1972)	90
83	Kentmere from High Street (1957)	91
84	Pillar Mountain from Fleetwith (1953)	93
85	Pillar Mountain from Fleetwith (Oils) (1955)	95
86	Sketch of Dounreay Nuclear Power Station (1954)	95
87	Dolphins and Merchild (1963)	96
88	Saint Bede (1904)	96
89	Poem (1965)	97
90	Breakthrough (1967)	97
91	Scafell Pike and Lingcove Beck (1967)	99
92	Harport (1982)	101
93	The Cullin and Loch Scavaig, Skye (1936)	103
94	Glen Lyon (1935)	104
95	Loch Clair and Liathach (1966)	106
96	Buchaille Etive Mhor (1982)	105
97	Lancet Peak, Ben Alder (1934)	107
98	Showers over Sgurr, Skye (1935)	107
99	Nordfjord and Hornelen, Norway (1968)	109
100	Night Fishers, Cassis, Provence (1925)	111
101	Temple of Aphaia, Aegina, Greece (1977)	112
102	Tulli (1983)	112
103	Haystacks, Monterchi, Italy (1968)	113
104	Dawn, Lake of Brienze (1952)	115
106	Mme Iréne Laure (1982)	117
107	Dr. Buchman and M. Robert Schuman at Caux (1948)	117
108	Caux and Montreux (1948)	118
109	Dent Du Midi from Caux (1948)	119
110	Down the Cumbrian Esk (1956)	121
111	The Flower of Understanding (1955)	123
112	Challenge (1969)	124
113	Madonna and Child (1973)	125
114	Ophelia (1967)	125
115	Quiet Pastures (1968)	127
116	Smörstabbre from Sognefjell, Norway (1962)	129
117	Victor Sparre (1982)	130
118	Evening Light, on Skagastolstinder (1976)	130
119	Appenine Village, Italy (1972)	131
120	Julian (1955)	132
121	Beach at Locarno (1983 by Julian Cooper)	132
122	Calle Nicaragua (under the Volcano) (by Julian Cooper (1982)	133
123	Fairfield from the North East (1973)	134
124	Morning Silver, Crummock (1980)	135
125	The Scafells from Needle Gully, Gable (1935)	137
126	Man (1964)	139
127	October in Langedalen, Norway (1968)	140
128	Evening Light, Rydal Water (1964)	141
129	Heaton beside Crummock Water (1983)	142

Introduction

Today I have enjoyed seven good hours of painting beside Wastwater and, on the way back over Wrynose and Hardknott Passes, I revelled in the richness and infinite variety of colours in the trees, in the valleys and in the golden-ochre grasses and rusty bracken that so thinly carpets the fells, with their purply-grey bones bursting through, revealing their anatomy and structure, and adding a note of wild strength to the scene.

It seems to be a good time to start out on the voyage of writing another book, one that might, I hope, go some way towards satisfying the many friends who have asked me to let them know what goes on beneath the surface of a life that has mostly been spent doing what I enjoy most – painting mountains.

This may seem to some people a somewhat limited aim in life. Perhaps my wants have been mostly small and limited, and yet there has always seemed to me to be some value in getting to know really well, in all its dimensions, one small part of our earth, in my case the Lake District in which I was born; not only the facts about it but also what I would call the 'inscape' – the spirit or character of one particular place to which the heart responds.

A Chinese painter and philosopher – the two activities often went together in China – whose name was Tsung Ping and who lived from 375 to 443 AD, wrote these words:–

> 'When the eyes respond and the mind agrees with the objects, the divine spirit may be felt, and truth may be attained in the painting.
>   Now the divine spirit has no trace, yet it dwells in each and every form and impresses it with its likeness'.
> *(Translated by Shio Sakaniski, Ph.D.)*

So that is why I am trying to put into words some of the motives that have underlain certain areas of my life and work.

Generally I find the medium of words a very difficult one by which to express infinite feelings, so I try to do it in paint. I suppose the fact is that one can never hope to express in either medium the whole truth that one sees, so I have set down as simply as I can what truth I do see.

Mischabel Range from Triffthorn, Swiss Alps
(1965)

SHEEP DIPPING AT NIBTHWAITE
(1968)

Around the end of the 18th century Thomas West, one of the early writers on the Lake District and author of 'Guide to the Lakes' chose as one of his 'stations' the fellside above High Nibthwaite, from which the visitor could obtain an approved view.

About the same time the painter and faithful delineator of the District, William Green, wrote about the great slate quarries in the heart of Coniston Old Man. Some 1100 tons of slate a year were being exported from Coniston at that time, and the first four miles of the journey were by water, off-loading at the stone quay at Nibthwaite for journeys as far away as to the West Indies.

From early childhood this south-east end of Coniton Water, first glimpsed from rare and exciting voyages on the Gondola, captained by one bearded Hamel, has held a fascination for me. The shore is a series of rocky promontories with a few islands, one, belonging to the Bridsons of Water Park, with a house on its rocky summit, and one of our discoveries was the hamlet of High Nibthwaite, its farms and barns and cottages nestling among the silurian rocks. From a rock immediately above the hamlet, I chose to paint a straightforward portrait of the place on a day in July when the annual dipping of the flocks was going on. I wish I could have a tape recording of the chorus of baa-ing from lambs and ewes that filled the air while I painted. The colour was simple – infinite variations of the greens of early summer showing between the warm greys of barn and wall and rocky outcrop. The day was one of diffused light which remained constant for many hours as I carried out this labour of the love I have always had for the sight and sound and smell of everything to do with sheep farming.

Chapter 1

Forbears

As I grow older, I realise more and more how much I owe to my parents. My father Alfred was born in 1863, the eldest of five children of an accountant in a cotton mill in Bolton, Lancashire, who had married one of the mill girls whose name was Alice. Alfred had been apprenticed as an accountant in the town hall by his father, but his heart was certainly not in it. It was in the kaleidoscope of skies that he could see through the town hall windows and, at weekends, in the great stretches of moorland that surround the Lancashire industrial towns, and in the old villages nestling in the wooded 'cloughs'. His mother understood and encouraged him in his paintings, though there was little encouragement for a budding painter in industrial Lancashire of the 1880s.

When Alfred was twenty one he sent some of his drawings and watercolours to the Westminster School of Art in London, was accepted as a student, and his mother persuaded her husband to allow Alfred to choose art as his profession. Earning a living in those conditions must have been a constant struggle for him; however, he built himself a small wooden studio close to his parents' house.

When he was twenty seven he saved up his pennies and went on a painting trip to Norway. He chose as his centre the village of Balholm, about half way up the Sogne Fjord, staying with the Kvikne family, who had then a small guest house, which, under the same ownership, has grown into a hotel with 400 bedrooms, and among the best in Norway, the land of good hotels. While he was in Balholm he met a girl, Mathilde Marie Valentinsen, who attracted him very deeply. He returned to Bolton, reviewed his prospects and wrote to Mathilde, asking her to be his wife in three years time, when he had saved up enough money. She was very definitely in love with Alfred and, very trustingly, said 'Yes, I will'.

Her father, Rasmus Valentinsen, had a tiny dyeing business in the village, and used only natural dyes that he obtained from mosses, bark, seaweeds and certain plants. In the spring, I can remember men with ruddy faces would come

Balholm and Ese Fjord, Norway (1966)

1

My Father (1907)

Fjaerlands Fjord, Norway (1966)

swooping down on skis, carrying on their backs great bundles of wool that their womenfolk had spun during the long dark winter months.

Mathilde was very popular in Balholm so the wedding was a great and romantic occasion for the village. The church stood at Tjugum, across half a mile of dark, mountain-girt Ese Fjord, and the wedding procession – the women in the colourful costumes of Sogn – rowed across the fjord and strolled up through the fields, accompanied by a fiddler, to the white church with lots of windows to let in the light and give views across the fjord.

As the bride and bridegroom left on the steamer for England some friends let off a few rockets as a farewell gesture. As it happened, they arrived in Newcastle on the night of November 5th, so they were welcomed by a good many more fireworks. The story goes that my mother said to my father, 'Isn't it nice that the English knew we were coming!'

My father was handsome, tall and fair, with long thick golden waving moustaches and a healthy rugged complexion. Even in his sixties he kept a vigorous muscular figure, for he just walked almost everywhere he went, except for long distances that involved trains. And he always carried a stout walking stick.

In complete contrast, my mother was rather short, with black hair and a rosy complexion. We imagined that, bearing such an unusual name for Norway, she must have descended from some unfortunate Spaniard that had been washed up after the defeat of the Armada. My mother was the practical member of the family. She ran the home well and economically, was always ready with a welcome, brought up her four children, two girls and two boys, in the way she had learnt through here own Lutheran upbringing. She had a real faith in God which she was able to pass on to her children and, at the same time, she partly believed in the existence of earth spirits that make the Norse folklore so vivid and real.

Both our parents attended the Anglican church each Sunday and we were all baptised and confirmed within the church, but we refused to attend Sunday school, considering that indoor worship once a week was quite enough. My father never spoke of his faith, though it was very real in his whole life. He lived for painting, and nature was his shrine. He spoke very sparingly to us, never punishing or even upbraiding us, (my mother made up for this very thoroughly!) and he enjoyed the company of his fellow men, relaxing over a glass of beer after walking, painting or following the hounds on foot over the fells. He particularly enjoyed the company of farmers and hunting folk, and regularly met his cronies each day in the snuggery of the Royal Oak Hotel in Ambleside.

Soon after coming to live in smoky Lancashire my mother developed severe bronchial ailments and was advised by her doctor to live somewhere that had mountain and sea air, otherwise she would not survive.

For this reason my parents came to live in the Lake District in 1898, first at Hawkshead and then at Coniston in a small cottage at Haws Bank with a delightful little garden and orchard. Then, after their daughter Ellide (named after a Norwegian ship) and Frithjof (named after an early Norse hero of Sogn) had been born, and I was on the way, they moved into a larger cottage which they named Solheim, 'the sunny home'. It is now Gate House as it is close by the gate of Holywath, the mansion of Coniston.

So that is where I was born on the sixth of October, 1903.

LEVERS WATER ABOVE CONISTON
(1960)

This was my first experience of a tarn, at the age of five. We had climbed Wetherlam, my first mountain top, and we ran down over grassy slopes and rock slabs to the welcoming water, stripped off all our clothes and splashed around in the icy-cold tarn.

On another occasion, I had been painting for hours beside the tarn and, when I had finished, I swam around, watching three of my friends walking along the skyline. Suddenly one of them detached himself and dropped like a hawk down the fellside. As I was drying myself in the sun, my friend and family doctor, Eric Fothergill, arrived running at great speed. He came to a halt in front of me and exploded with anger, mixed with well-concealed relief.

Apparently, from the ridge, he had seen me plunge into the tarn but failed to see me emerge round a rocky headland, and had assumed the worst.

The day of the painting was one of those hazy sunny days of early spring that seemed timeless in that hanging valley among the mountains of my childhood, which still held the power to fill me with awe and wonder mixed with an intense desire to explore every crag and hollow. Against the hazy sunlight the great rock became a presence, so dark against the shadows in the fellside that grew paler towards the skyline.

The colours that day were very simple, all atmospheric, the sunlight palest gold and the distant slopes, becoming yellow ochre down by the margin of the tarn, and warmer and more umber in the foreground.

Before mining operations began in this combe above Coniston, it must have been quite the grandest and rockiest in the Lake District, at the southern edge of the volcanic rock where it steps down 2000 feet to the surrounding areas of silurian rock, with a narrow band of mountain limestone running through it.

The mines in the combe below were probably explored for copper in Roman times, but it was in 1561 that a Germany company from Augsburg opened up there on a large scale, mining copper and lead, for only eighty-five years. They were opened up again in 1848, when five or six hundred men were employed. The deep crack in the rocks at the foot of the tarn is named Simon's Nick after one Simon who discovered a rich vein of copper. As children we found these mine workings far more exciting than mere unspoilt fellsides.

Chapter 2

Parents

At that time my parents were having great difficulty in earning enough money to feed their growing family, and I suspect that sometimes they went without their necessary food themselves. A nearby wood and the open fellside were our nurseries and, of course, we had no toys other than what we made ourselves. The house abutted a fairly fast beck that came down from the Old Man and Wetherlam, well over 2,000 feet above. After rain we were frightened and thrilled to hear great boulders bumping against the foundations. This early association with Mines Beck and running water and the love of it has meant a great deal to me all my life, and it was very greatly the lack of it that was almost unbearable in later years in London, and later still in Sussex. In fact the earliest memory I have, from about the age of three, is sitting beside the beck near our home, dipping one of my father's old brushes in the clear running water and spreading it over a rounded green boulder veined with lines of white quartz. My first effort at painting.

One day when I was only a few months old and my father was out painting, a man called to see him from a firm of London publishers, Adam and Charles Black. Little Ellide managed to find my father, who was offered a commission to carry out 75 illustrations for a forthcoming large colour book, 'The English Lakes', to be written by W. T. Palmer, a journalist. They offered him £3 for the copyright of each painting, which meant that my father had no royalties if it succeeded.

My Mother, Ellide, Frithjof and Myself (1908)

My Family at our Home at Balholm (1907)

Autumn Flames, Norway (1968)

The commission had arrived just in time to be the turning point of the family's fortunes. My father eagerly tramped all over the district at all times of year and in all kinds of weather, producing a series of paintings that, in reproduction, have the power to delight people to this day.

The first edition, including 500 de luxe autographed numbered copies in large format, bound in white and gold, came out in 1905, and was an immediate success. The colour plates, printed in Germany, were good, and each plate was protected by tissue paper.

The effect of all this on my father was, perhaps, not surprising in a man of such optimism and enterprise. He immediately ordered from Jacob Digre of Trondhjem, in Norway, a large studio built of whole trunks of pine, numbered and fitted so well that no inner wall was needed. This cost him the great sum of £150, and the cost of transport from Newcastle to Coniston exceeded this sum. He had it erected in the middle of the village, and hung the walls with his paintings, selling them to visitors if he wasn't out painting them.

It was a brilliant stroke of business and succeeded so well that, the very next year, he ordered a two-storied wooden house from the same builder, and had it built at Balholm, a few yards from the edge of the fjord. He fondly imagined that the whole family would spend a part of each year at Balholm, but funds did not run so far as this, so, in a few years it was sold. Strangely enough it is still called Cooperhus, even in the plan of the village that has now become Balestrand. However, we all spent a glorious fifteen months in it over the years 1906 – 1908 and we even possessed a splendid rowing boat made in the village.

Back in Coniston all three children went to the village school until it became obvious that such education was not sufficient, so we moved into part of a Georgian house in Princes Street, Ulverston, a pleasant market town that contained a grammar school as well as a preparatory school.

My father used to take the train to Coniston each morning, occasionally walking back the fourteen miles in the evening.

One memory I have of that period was of being persuaded to wear a reindeer skin suit, with hat, long coat, leggings and turned-up-toed boots, all edged with red and blue felt. My father had brought it from Norwegian Lapland. I had worn it first in Balholm on the occasion of the visit of the Norwegian Royal Family, King Haakon, Queen Maud and the Crown Prince Olav, who is the same age as myself and was also wearing a skin suit just like mine. The Queen noticed this and graciously received a bunch of roses from my tiny hands. I wonder if Norway's splendid King Olav still remembers his visit to Balholm.

While we were living in Ulverston, my mother's younger sister, Otalia Valentinsen, came from Norway to live with us and to help my mother with the growing family. We children all loved her deeply. She was devoted to us and, possibly because she was stone deaf, she made more allowances for us than did my mother. She continued to live with or near to our family until her death in 1941 when living in a small cottage in Langdale.

In her memory, and because we liked the name Otalia, my wife and I called our first born after her.

FEBRUARY SNOWS IN LITTLE LANGDALE (1983)

It was one of those rare days of anti-cyclonic weather in February of this year, with hardly any wind, hours of sunlight and the newly fallen snow adding great height and liveliness to the fells, drawing the eye of the beholder up to the summits.

When I looked out of my window at 6.30am I knew where to go, but various duties kept me back, and it was after ten by the time I settled down to paint, just about half-an-hour too late. This being so, I made a swift wash and crayon sketch of the blue shadows in the snow, including the shadow cast by Wetherlam on the hanging valley of Greenburn below the crags of Carrs, and the rounded slopes of Wet Side Edge that fall down to Wrynose Pass.

Having done that in half an hour, I made a careful chalk drawing of the whole subject on paper 22'' by 15'', using blue chalks and violet in the distances, and umber and black towards the foreground. The conditions on the following day were precisely the same by 9.30 – a very rare occurrence in the Lake District – so I was able to start immediately on the sky and the shadows on the fells, taking the blue right over the lower ground not covered with snow. Next came the half-tones of cobalt with a little more vermilion, and of course, much paler, suggesting the forms of the mountains, the blues becoming deeper towards the nearer valley.

After all the shadows were painted and dry, I started on the areas not covered in snow, first the sparse rocks in the gullies and ribbs of Carrs, then the higher and farther reaches of Wetherlam, and, lower down, the warmer slopes of bracken and grass, leading to the golden green of the fields and the cadmium-orange rushes around the edges of the tarn. There was a slight breeze on the water that produced blurred vertical bands among the many horizontal forms.

The nearer trees and the lumps of earth in the foreground were painted in earth colours, mixed with ultramarine in the shadows.

From here, the valley and tarn and fells all came together in a natural composition, a lovely place seen under ideal conditions.

Chapter 3

Childhood

Frithjof (1926)

It was in Ulverston in 1908 that a second daughter, Una Mathilde, was born, thus completing our family of two boys and two girls. I was very fond of them all, especially of my brother Frithjof, who was very steady and calm under all circumstances. I was the direct opposite, flying into outrageous tempers if I could not have my way, even to the extent of throwing chairs at whoever frustrated me. Frithjof would quietly sit on me until my temper subsided.

In 1911 we all moved back again towards the centre of the Lake District, to Ambleside. My enterprising father moved the log studio piece by piece to a site he rented on the corner of Lake Road and Wansfell Road, moving it once more, in 1928, to a site he bought half way between the village and the Lake. We lived in a pleasant house in Millans Park with a garden that sloped down to the playing field of the Kelsick Grammar School.

The school itself was situated nearly a mile from the village up a steep hill on the side of Wansfell, and didn't that hill seem steep when the school bell was ringing and I had the several steepest hundreds of yards still to run! I suppose we ought to feel grateful for the governors of the school for choosing that site, for it certainly developed the leg muscles which, in my case, proved useful later in following the hounds on foot for miles over the fells, for fell walking and, later, for rock climbing, and in the only fell race I ever entered, when I managed to stagger in fourth.

My brother Frithjof went with me to the Grammar School, the girls to a Parents National Education Union School that has now become the Charlotte Mason College of Education, named after the founder of the P.N.E.U. method.

The most vivid memories I have of those school days was of fierce battles, sometimes in single combat with fists, at others in gangs that were formed on the flimsiest excuses for combat, such as British versus Romans or Royalists versus Roundheads. These wars, sometimes lasting for a whole term, would involve the use of ammunition such as acorns or even stones, one side ambushing the other among the many outcrops of rock and the oak woods that enriched the country to each side of the school road.

On the north side of the road was the deep gorge of Stock Beck, crowned at the top by a splendid waterfall, Stock Ghyll. Some of us formed a club, the entrance test of which was to leap from stone to stone up the gorge. The waterfall was divided near the top by a rocky island and, nestling in it, was a small beach of sandy gravel. The final test for the would-be member was to jump across the waterfall on to the shingly beach, and his reward was a cigar made from brown paper. You see, we were able to smoke there in safety.

Fairyland of Snow, Rydal (A. Heaton Cooper, 1927)

Blencathra from Guard House (1971)

The vicar of Ambleside at that time was a jovial Irishman, John Hawksworth. He and his imposing but kind wife had seven sons, all of whom went on to St Bees, the public school on the Cumberland coast, and on to the Queen's College, Oxford, so that anyone could date these two establishments for many years by which Hawksworth was there. My best friends were the twins, Desmond and Geoffrey, who were both good at games. I was very bad at having to do with any object moving at speed, yet, in spite of this and of my unheeded pleadings to the head, I was elected captain of the cricket for one season and I had hardly ever before endured such prolonged misery.

I was confirmed into the Anglican church at the early age of eleven in order to be 'done' at the same time as Frithjof, my fourteen-year-old brother. The experience of willingly committing myself to following Christ all my life was, for me, a very important and emotional one, and I can remember the tears pouring down my face as Bishop Diggle of Carlisle laid his hands on my head.

Unknown to me, but possibly not to my parents, the vicar walked the eight miles to Coniston to persuade Mrs Barratt, my godmother who lived at Holywath, Coniston, to offer to pay for my education at a public school and at a university on one condition, that I should become a minister of the Church of England.

It never occurred to me at that time to question this kind, although conditional, offer, so I got to work to win the entrance examination to St Bees. Our headmaster, the Reverend Francis Lewis, was himself a clergyman, and he generously gave many hours of his time after school to coaching three of us boys in Greek. Latin was part of the school's normal curriculum. The result was that we all gained scholarships, thanks to the head and the very patient staff.

I was thirteen by this time and, during the holidays and in all spare time, I would be drawing everything I saw, especially the trees, mountains and farms. This occupation grew steadily and ever more strongly, being fed all the time by the example of my father, whom I always loved and admired. He never, as far as I can remember, seemed to notice my efforts until the great day came when he gave me a paintbox, brushes and paper, and asked me to go out painting with him. The subject he had chosen was a very difficult one to interpret in watercolour, being a stretch of the River Brathay above Skelwith Force, with a tangle of pussy-palms, willows and rushes reflected in the flowing river, and I did not do very well.

From then onwards I was entirely gripped by the urge to put down in colour all the things and places that I loved, and, the stronger this urge, the stronger came my doubts about a public school, university and the inevitable church.

Codale Tarn (A. Heaton Cooper, 1927)

I was very much aware of how much my parents cared for me and wanted the best for my life, and they could never have afforded the cost of an education such as was being offered, yet my heart was not in it, and it was being pulled very strongly towards painting and working with my father, who, I could see very clearly, was completely happy and fulfilled in his work and his way of life.

Finally, after several days with him and alone on the fells, I plucked up courage to tell my father and mother that I was not going to be a parson, but a painter.

I don't know what sort of opposition I had been dreading, but I was completely astonished when they both showed how delighted they were about my decision.

All through his painting life my father was very definitely of the 'plein air' school of landscape painters, those who believed in painting mostly, or totally, out-of-doors in front of the subject. This, of course, is particularly difficult in the ever-changing light and mood of Britain, compared with the steadier weather conditions in France, especially the south, and it was on the French painters, first of all the Barbizon school and later on the French impressionists, particularly Claude Monet, that my father relied for his inspiration and encouragement. And, of course, all through his painting life he was training his visual memory to enable him to continue working on a painting either on the spot or in his studio, and to produce a water colour in full colour and tone from the flimsiest note in a sketch book.

I often thought that he worked too long on a watercolour, striving to attain the strength of an oil painting instead of allowing the white paper to show through the washes of watercolour, but in this I could well have been mistaken, for, in his best and later work, he retained both delicacy and strength.

CLIMBERS IN EASTER GULLY, DOW CRAG, (1924)

Dow Crag, at 2555 feet above sea level, forms the western half, of which Coniston Old Man is the eastern half, of the combe that holds the wildest, rockiest tarn in the Lake District – Goats Water. As I had been born at the foot of these fells, they became our playground and the scene of many youthful adventures among the crags, and of exciting discoveries of the signs of inhabitation by the Britons 4000 years ago.

As one looks at Dow Crag from the Old Man, five buttresses form the main rock wall. Climbers have called them 'A', (the most southerly one), 'B', 'C', 'D' and 'E' (the most northerly one). The buttresses are separated by gullies or by chimneys, the widest, Great Gully, between 'A' and 'B' buttresses and the next widest, Easter Gully, between 'D' and 'E'. Some 50 feet above the foot of the crag and above a great chockstone, the gully broadens out into a rock-strewn amphitheatre, from which radiate a number of buttresses, walls and chimneys. Counting from left to right, the first one is Blizzard Chimney, which the three climbers in the painting are starting to ascend.

They are Gordon Osmaston, his wife June and myself. It was a gloriously sunny day in September, the sunlit golden grasses and light rocks on the Old Man casting a warm reflected light into our gully, Goats Water beneath and Coniston Water beyond introducing contrasting notes of blue into the landscape.

For this, I made a detailed pencil drawing in my sketchbook and recalled the tones, colours and figures at leisure in my studio. We managed several climbs that day, finishing with Intermediate Gully. It was almost dark when we arrived on the summit of Dow Crags and our mood of achievement and wonder was immensely heightened and deepened by watching the last after-sunset glow over the sea to the west.

16

Chapter 4

Youth

At that time World War I had been raging for three years, yet so immune from it were we that the only effect, beside what we read in the papers, that it had upon our family was that my father joined the Volunteer Training Corps, a sort of Home Guard, my sister Ellide went to do war work on the east coast, and my brother Frithjof lied about his age and joined the Royal Flying Corps at the age of 17, returning with wounds after two years service.

After leaving school at fourteen, my life was entirely and happily filled with doing odd jobs about my father's studio, such as laying and tending the log fire that burned on the flat hearth of the great chimney, carved from soapstone from the mason's yard at Trondhjem Cathedral; mounting and framing watercolours, and attending to callers when my father was out, and, on very special occasions, going out painting with my father in some new and exciting part of the Lake District. Occasionally I would go off by myself for a few days, ranging the fells and drawing and painting all the way, staying in farms in Wasdale, Eskdale, Dunnerdale or Buttermere.

One December, when I was about fifteen, I read in the daily paper that Mars would approach close to Earth, and that there might be violent storms on our planet, especially on December 17th. On the night of the 16th storms began to build up to dramatic proportions. I mentioned this rather casually to my father, but he did not seem to be interested. Early on the 17th I woke up to find a very violent storm of wind and rain was almost shaking the house. This convinced me that it signalled the end of the world. I decided to have a front seat view of this unique occasion, so I cycled seven miles up Langdale, climbed, with considerable buffetings, to the top of the Langdale Pikes and crouched behind a rock, as the wind was too strong to let me stand up, waiting for the climax.

Suddenly the wind and rain stopped, the sun burst out between the storm clouds, flooding the valley with light, and sparkling on all the thousands of new rivulets. For me, this experience was just as though I and everyone else had died, and somehow had been miraculously brought to life again.

Rapids on the Esk (1956)

East Buttress, Scafell (1936)

I went down on my knees and thanked God for His world and His deliverance.

This experience, and another when I was seventeen, made indelible marks on my life. I had been painting alone half way up Wansfell, looking up towards the Coniston fells on an afternoon of showers interspersed with shafts of golden sunlight. Finally I gave up painting in despair, and just continued to watch the showers falling on the central fells, the sparkling rivulets and the River Brathay flowing into Windermere and down to the sea, and the sun licking up moisture from the sea, while the west wind carried great banks of cloud back again to the mountains.

Something about this orderly cycle of the movement of the waters suddenly filled me with inexpressible wonder and delight. I knew then, for myself, that there was a mind responsible for the design and creation of the universe, including myself. For hours I stayed there in ecstasy, and this feeling stayed with me for many days and weeks. It occurred again at periods during my life, but never again quite as vividly as at that first time.

When I was about seventeen I had been helping with the Ambleside Water Carnival at the head of Windermere on a cold rainy, windy, August day, got drenched through, had an enormous tea and then dived into the lake to reach a board tied to the back of a motor boat to perform an early form of water skiing, but, not suprisingly, I got cramp before I could stand on the board, and went under. As I was going down for the third time a friend, Norman Gatey, who was in the motor boat, dived into the lake in his mackintosh and even wearing his trilby hat, and fished me out, for which noble deed he was awarded the medal of the Royal Humane Society.

On three days a week I would cycle the thirteen miles into Kendal to attend the Kendal Art School. Its principal, Philip W. Holyoake, never tried to teach me anything, for he soon realised who was my true master, though he would sometimes criticise my work constructively, my efforts to paint stuffed birds in the nearby museum, to draw in pastel scenes in Kendal and to draw in pencil and charcoal various pyramids, cubes and spheres and very dead-white casts from Greek sculpture, an activity of which Cézanne would have approved. There was no life class.

It was some of these drawings from the antique, as well as from natural landscape, that, at the age of nineteen, enabled me to gain a five year scholarship at the Royal Academy Schools of Painting. I had never before been in any city, and the experience of London was quite overwhelming and secretly very disappointing as I viewed it with my father from Hungerford Bridge on our first evening. The London of my imagination had been a city of magnificent buildings such as those shown in books on London – and a city that could be seen as whole from some eminence, much as Athens can be seen from the surrounding hills.

The first room I had was with an Alsatian poet, Victor Plarr, and his family in Wimbledon. Victor held the post of librarian at the Royal College of Surgeons, but his real life centred on the Poetry Society and the verse of his friends Dowden and Swinburne. However, as I was expected to be in to dinner at seven, and this meant cutting part of the life class, I soon moved to a room of my own in Wellington Square, off Kings Road, Chelsea, which cost me ten shillings and sixpence a week.

I made a painting in gouache of my bed sitting room, genuinely Victorian, and exhibited it with the Royal Society of British Artists some years later, where it was sold.

The Royal Academy Schools are situated at the back of Burlington House in Piccadilly, and the only approach to them is from Burlington Gardens, down a narrow dark alley behind high black walls, in which we students would play a sort of cricket in lunch hours.

At that time I was a painfully self-conscious youth, only too aware of my long thin body and constantly red nose, and of my colossal ignorance of art and, indeed, of everything remotely connected with this new life. I had done only one oil painting at home in my life, a small one of Oaks Farm, Ambleside, and all painting in the school was in oil, none in watercolour or tempera.

There was no tuition in the technique of painting other than occasional sessions with the Keeper. The Keeper at that time was Charles Sims, R.A., who

Kern Knotts Chimney, Gable (1934)
Scafell from Mickledore (1935)

was an intensely shy, retiring soul, and one was always aware of the tortures of self-consciousness he was suffering. His work seemed to me clever but lacking in content. In later years he suddenly started painting abstracts. Sad to say, he eventually took his own life.

Undoubtedly, the most helpful part of the curriculum was the life class for drawing in the evenings. Here was a medium with which I was already slightly familiar, leaving me free to concentrate on the problem of interpreting three-dimensional living form on a two-dimensional piece of paper by means of pencil or conté chalk.

Added to this was the presence of one of the finest drawing masters in Britain, Ernest Jackson. He had his own philosophy of life that came out in his teaching. He would sit down beside a student, talk upon life in general and, meanwhile, his pencil had been drawing – perhaps an arm or a leg, just two simple boundary lines and a slight shading that showed variations of thickness or bone structure. His master was Raphael.

Jackson realised some of the tortures of inability I had been undergoing, and he advised me not to try to express the whole truth about the figure in one session. Truth, he said, is rather like a diamond with an infinite number of facets. No one can see all of them. 'You may see a few this evening. I can see possibly a few more. Be content with putting down on the paper, as simply as you can, what truth you do see. Then go home, have a good sleep, come back tomorrow and see more facets. The important thing is that you continue to learn, and add to your understanding of truth'.

I am glad to say that, in the church of St James, Piccadilly, known as the artists' church, there is a memorial tablet to Jackson and a painting of his, placed there by a number of his grateful pupils.

To me at that time it seemed that all the students knew far more about art than I did, and this was probably quite true. The effect was to make me very reserved,

and I was surprised to learn, years later, that I had the reputation of appearing the most 'superior' student of my time.

One student, Patrick Millard, had family connections with Cumberland. He saw through my mask of superiority and he would take considerable pains to jockey me out of some misery and to befriend me, for which I have always been grateful. In later life Pat Millard was principal of the St John's Wood Art School, and, eventually, principal of Goldsmiths' College of Art, which is part of London University. His reign at Goldsmiths was so successful that, after his death, the new addition to the College was named Millard Hall.

Gradually I thawed out with other students. There was the Russian, Alexander Bilibin, the son of a distinguished designer for the theatre who stayed on after the 1917 revolution while his wife and two sons emigrated to London: Edwin John, son of Augustus John, who could draw the figure superbly. I took Edwin one evening to the gymnasium of the Honourable Artillery Corps in Bunhill Row in the city. He became very keen on boxing and took it up, some years later, as a profession, intending to earn a lot of money quickly, which would enable him to follow the profession of art independently of his famous father.

Then there was George Lambourn, whose father was a grocer in Rotherhithe in the east end of London. He disapproved of his son's choice of a career and would not allow him enough money for his bus fare and something to eat during the day. Most of us considered 'Mike' Lambourn to be the best painter among us at that time and we conspired to help in various ways. When I had a studio in Sussex I invited him to come and stay for a weekend any time. He walked the 56 miles, stayed for five weeks and, at the end of it, married an heiress, Joan Waterlow, of the great printing family, and eventually he became a landowner.

Although we didn't see him often after he was a past student, I always got on well with Ivon Hitchens. Once, after watching me painting on an oil of Troutbeck, without asking for information he took the train to Staveley, a rather dull village near Kendal. In the morning he looked out of the hotel window and took the first train back to London. I consider Hitchens to be one of the finest landscape painters in Britain today, as his work seems to me to express

Evening, Thirlmere (1964)

22

in colour, tone and simple painterly form the inner feeling of England's landscape, and, at the same time, create a new thing of richness and bold expressive brushwork.

At the R.A. Schools there was a system whereby each Royal Academician is allowed to visit the schools for a month to give instruction to the students. Several used to come, but we used to consider them rather 'fuddy duddy'. When Russel Flint tried to teach us he became so embarrassed that we were rather sorry for him, yet, in later life, he was at ease in any company and became a real charmer. George Clausen, ruddy-cheeked and white of hair, was like a breath of fresh country air. We found him rather difficult, however, as he invariably started painting on a canvas already half painted by a student, and, besides, flung the brushes all over the floor as he used each one once.

By far the most helpful in my time was Walter Sickert. He gave us strange advice sometimes, such as to choose a photograph in a daily picture paper, square it up on a canvas, paint it it Indian Red monochrome, and, finally, in colours from imagination. Even Sickert had the disconcerting habit of completely rearranging the model whom we had been painting on for several days. But he was a painter and we knew it. One day as I was painting the head of a model, experimenting in pure colours, Sickert looked at the canvas – 'Very good', he said. 'Very good. But what if the model had been wearing a kilt. You would have used up all your purest colours on his head and you'd have nothing left for his tartan'.

REFLECTIONS, THIRLMERE (1936)

Before painting, I watched the play of cloud shadows over the landscape and chose for my painting a moment when the foreground was in sunlight, the middle distance in cloud shadow and the distance in light, fixing this combination in my memory and translating whatever happened later into this theme. I then proceed to paint very swiftly and directly.

It was a still morning in February, and, at that time of year, there was no evaporation from the standing waters, so the blues of the sky were clear cobalt, turning to green-blue towards the horizon by the addition of a little aureolin yellow. The clouds were slightly warmer and not so white as the distant snows – palest light red and the snows pure white paper – and all this repeated in reverse, though darker, in the lake, with a little burnt sienna added to the cobalt in the nearer water.

The purplish and reddish browns of the winter woodlands, ochres and warm greens of the grasses and the warm greys of the rocks were painted directly and full strength on to dry paper, as were the blue grey cloud shadows of the middle distance, becoming warmer and darker in the nearer shadowed woods, some nearer trees with a touch of Winsor blue added to the cobalt and light red. All these tones were reflected in deeper tones in the lake, and painted with horizontal strokes to suggest slight movement. The darkest shadows of the foreground were painted in variations of ultramarine mixed with burnt sienna or alizarin crimson.

The training of visual memory, of course, is the key to painting out-ot-doors, especially in the ever changing light of the British Isles.

Chapter 5

Sussex

During the first two years in London I felt an increasing sense of pressure. Everything was so close, there was nowhere where I could focus on any distance and rest my eyes, only dark city streets. I had, too, a yearning to be free of all restraint and authority, and a strong desire to see running and falling water. This may derive from the fact that I was born in a cottage beside a beck. I have had this feeling all my life.

After two years of London I was invited by an older student, Dennis Earle, whom I did not know very well, to spend a weekend with some of his friends in Sussex.

At that time my father was enjoying a modest amount of success and, all through my student days, he sent me £2 a week. When I left the R.A. Schools after only two years instead of five, quite rightly this allowance stopped. In my second year I won the Creswick Prize for Landscape, the subject being 'Sky clearing after rain', which brought me in £30 a year for three years. I exhibited and sold oil paintings at the Royal Academy Summer Exhibitions and the Goupil Gallery, so an occassional sale, together with the Creswick Prize, provided almost enough for my needs. While a student, I had a model apse made in plaster, and painted on it in tempera an Ascension with apostles. Later this was bought by John Oxenham, the writer of books and hymns.

Another painting, of my earlier Chelsea bed sitter, was purchased by Dr Wood of Enfield who, when I lunched with him, showed me round his very Catholic collection of paintings which included a Rembrandt and a Paul Nash.

When I was sharing one of the Stamford Bridge studios with Dennis we decided one day that we both needed new flannel trousers. Our combined finances did not run to two pairs, so we went to the Scotch House in Knightsbridge and asked an astonished assistant to measure us both for one pair of trousers, wide enough for Dennis and long enough for me. Unfortunately Dennis's build was short and thick and mine long and thin. The result in practice was that, when he wore them, the tops reached half way up his chest and, when I did, I had to tuck them in folds round my waist.

One October Dennis and I went to Paris, mainly to see paintings. I was captivated especially by the dramatic 'Massacre of Scio', by Delacroix, and his paintings of fighting horses and lions. But the painter who most interested me was Cézanne. The first painting by Cézanne that moved me deeply was his 'La Maison du Pendu', in which the solid forms – almost sculptural in their three dimensional realisation – satisfied me in the same way as do great mountain forms in their design.

Cézanne's absolute integrity in his search for truth and his vigorous expression of his vision place him among the great masters. He reacted against the influence of his contemporaries among the Impressionists, saying of Monet 'He is nothing but an eye. But what an eye!'

About his own work he said. 'There are two things in the painter: the eye and the brain. The two must co-operate: one must work for the development of both, but as a painter: of the eye, through the outlook on nature: of the brain, through the logic of organised sensations which provide the means of expression.'

He was greatly misunderstood and unappreciated by most of his contemporaries, and he found relationships among his family and friends often difficult, so that, in his later years, his life was embittered and isolated. Indeed, so complex a character was Cézanne that students of his life and work continue to find new interpretations and meanings, especially in his powerful imaginative compositions, such as the many versions of the theme of the bathers.

Cézanne looked at nature for its own sake, devoid of any literary, romantic or illusionist associations. His paintings were architectural constructions, obeying only laws within themselves, conveying space and perspective by colour alone. So it was that he opened the way for future painters to be free to produce works that were objects in themselves, without depending upon anything outside themselves. And, in his landscapes, he remained faithful to his beloved Provence, the country in which he was born.

Only he among the moderns was able to express the rhythmic inter-relationship of solid forms, as though carved in paint, his colour expressing each facet of his forms, his trees well rooted in the earth and springing upward against the force of gravity, everything in the Provençal sunlight reflecting colour from

Eagles Nest, Gable (1937)

Les Calanques, Provence (1925)

earth and sky. His many studies of Mont Sainte Victoire under different conditions fascinated me and I vowed to see my native mountains as he did. The work of André Derain interested me also at that time.

One day we decided to go on to Marseilles, a railway journey which cost us the equivalent of £1, and from there we used to walk out early in the morning eastwards along the coast, and paint among the wonderful calanques – creeks of blue-green water surrounded by sheer white limestone cliffs, with fishing villages at the heads of the creeks. It was on these cliffs near his home that Gaston Rébuffat, the great French mountaineer, served his apprenticeship to rock. We nearly had to live in one of the caves in the cliffs, but a cheque for one of my paintings, sold in London, enabled us to hitch on to Cassis.

The brilliant light of Provence was a revelation to me. I was intoxicated with the light and colour and tones, and painted all hours, even at night on the quay, with a more highly-pitched range of colours than I had ever used for landscape. The experience helped me to love Van Gogh more than ever. It was very good to be painting the same country and in the same light that he and Cézanne had painted, the same rocks and pines and vineyards.

But when it came to painting the changing fleeting light of my native Cumbria, I found I needed an approach that was both more swiftly impressionist and, at the same time, more imaginative and 'spiritual', in the way it was linked with my own spiritual experience and, anyway, it was my own country.

Sometime around 1927 there was held, during the winter in the Royal Academy, a magnificent exhibition of Chinese Art. This was a revelation to me, especially the paintings of landscape, trees, birds and still or falling water, and especially the art of the Sung and Ming dynasties – Ma Yuan among the mountains and rivers; Hsia Kuei with his long scroll of a thousand miles of the Yangtse River; Emperor Hui Tsang and, among the 16th century painters, Yen Tung Ko with his 'Birds returning through a snowy sky'. Anyone who could so well understand the rhythmic pattern of a flock of birds in flight must indeed be great.

At the same time, at the Burlington Gallery there was an exhibition of contemporary Chinese paintings in the great tradition of Chinese art. I was the only person in the gallery except Professor Liu Hai Su, Professor of Art at Shanghai University. We conversed in French and he revealed to me a great deal about the Chinese mind, its humility towards nature and art, especially painting.

Grey Crags, Buttermere (1936)

The Sanctuary Garden (1925)

Grey Crag,
Birkness
Coombe

There were some superb examples of his own work in the exhibition, yet this great artist had put aside a year of his life in order to take this exhibition of his fellow artists' work around many of the capitals of the world.

I was especially attracted by the Chinese attitude towards the place of man in nature, humbly taking his small place among the rest of creation. This attitude of humility is especially evident in the work of painters of the Sung dynasty – Fan Kuan in his painting of a man sitting in contemplation by a stream, Tung Pei-Yuan in his 'Secluded villa'. They are both magnificent mountain paintings.

The place in Sussex where, eventually, I built my studio was an area of 30 acres of sandy ground with woodlands of pine. It had been bought by a lovely Irish girl named Vera Pragnell. Her father had been a general in the British army and her mother lived in London. Vera, at the age of around 25, became disillusioned with social life in the 1920s and decided to try an experiment in sociology.

She let it be known, through her many friends in every walk of life, that anyone, whosoever they were, could have half an acre of land, provided they came to work and live on it. She called it the Sanctuary. At the start the only building there was an eighteenth century pair of cottages knocked into one, built of brick and timber, the living room used as a general meeting place, the bedrooms for guests, and, at one end, a tiny chapel. There was a garden of vegetables and flowers which Vera worked, herself living in a wooden hut about 10 feet by 8 feet near the cottage. She was fairly tall, with thick red-gold hair and the Irish complexion that goes with it, humorous grey-blue eyes and a large generous mouth. She intensely enjoyed being alive, radiating joy and delight. I fell in love with her at first sight.

As was to be expected, the Sanctuary attracted a very varied lot of people. One of the most delightful of these was a gentle old man, George Mann, who carved wood happily in his ancient high caravan. Then there was a poet and his family, and a gardener named Dan Huxtep, one of the founders of the National Union of Agricultural Workers. Every Easter, Dan would open up his plot of land to a camp of members of the Young Communist League, who behaved very correctly, and held sing-songs round a camp fire each night. One of them, Fred Vickery, who had worked in a match factory, decided to come and live at the Sanctuary. He built himself a wooden hut, cultivated a good vegetable garden and earned a living locally by building henhouses.

I asked him to build me a studio. It measured 20 feet by 15 feet and had a six foot square rooflight and a window 10 feet by 6 feet with a wide window sill that I used for my bed. I made a canvas awning that extended from the window, and I slept under it in the summer. One problem was the nightingales that kept me awake at night. The furniture consisted of a table, two chairs, an easel and three triangular shelves in a corner to hold food, pots and pans and an oil cooking stove.

In April 1928 the 'Studio' magazine then the élite of British art magazines, published an article about me and my work. One of the five illustrations – one of them being in colour, was a watercolour of Vera and myself working in the garden of the Sanctuary cottage. It was in this garden that I first built my studio, later moving it on to the open heath. This was the only time in my life at which I lived almost entirely off my vegetable produce.

I used to paint on the downs and among the chalk pits and forests, revelling in the freedom from gloomy London and the R.A. Schools, but exhibiting and selling my work in London galleries, such as the R.A., the R.B.A. and the Goupil Gallery.

Upper Eskdale (1971)

The Sanctuary was a meeting place for all kinds of people. Sometimes the

30

'county' would call on Vera and find themselves dancing folk dances with young communists or artists of some ilk. The trouble was that they all, in their own ways, fell in love with Vera.

I was very impressed by the unity of purpose, close fellowship and discipline of Dan Huxtep and his communist friends, but it worried me to know that they would never achieve the new world they were longing for as long as they denied God. Here was splendid material heading in the wrong direction. While I was, myself, a rebel against the evils of capitalism, I knew that communism was not the answer, but I didn't known what was.

One day my brother Frithjof turned up with a tent and not much else. He told me he had given up his job in the progress department of the Fairey Aviation Company at Hayes in Middlesex, and was looking for a more simple, peaceful life. But Frithjof was never by nature a very peaceful person, and, at some time in his life, he had become strongly anti-communist, even going so far as to help the British Fascists to break the general strike of 1926.

One night at Easter, as I was fast asleep, he crept into my studio and whispered, "Heat, have you got a black stocking?" I asked him, "What on earth for?" He told me that he was going to take down the red flag flying on a tall pole in the middle of the young communists' camp. I turned over without a word, but I couldn't get to sleep for thinking of what would happen if, or rather when, they caught him.

Eventually I put on a long ancient driving coat, given me by a friend of my father, and walked along in the moonlight to the camp. All was quiet, the flag was still flying so I walked about for a while smoking a cigarette, then, as nothing happened, I returned to bed. I was almost asleep when Frithjof arrived. 'What happened?' I asked. 'Well', he said, 'I crept up to the hedge near the camp, but there was a guard in a long dark coat walking about smoking, so I had to give it up'.

At this time I painted a half-figure of Christ for the chapel. He was seen as a young strong man against a background of a Sussex wood at sunrise. When, in later years, I saw Piero della Francesca's Resurrection in his birthplace, Borgo San Sepolcro, I realised that was really what I was trying to paint, that all-powerful presence, here and now.

That summer I took Vera home for a few days to meet my parents, but it was far from a success, as neither side took to each other.

When I returned to Sussex in October, Vera told me that she and Dennis were to be married, and they asked if I would be the best man. The marriage took place at Marylebone Registry Office. I decided to leave the Sanctuary never to return, in spite of many requests from Vera and Dennis. When their daughter, Deirdre, was born I agreed to be her godfather, and kept in touch for all too few years.

THE ROCKY SHORE OF
WASTWATER (1972)

Here is one of the exquisite parts of Wastwater's shoreline that came within a hairsbreadth of being destroyed when the lake was threatened with being turned into a reservoir in 1981. The whole affair was one of the cases in which conservation was achieved through sheer love and appreciation on the part of many individuals, and through them, to conservation societies, pitted against a powerful nuclear combine backed by the government. Truly, David and Goliath!

I firmly believe that this form of conservation, through gentle persuasion and education, can be more effective, in the long term, than violent and sometimes anti-human demonstrations. Perhaps the situation is critical enough to require both ways.

Here, in the foreground, are two layers of rounded slabs, one laid upon the other as the layers of volcanic ash cooled into rock. Then came the ice that left the upper surfaces in curving wave-like forms, while frost and water power revealed the vertical cleavage of each layer.

Across the lake, the screes fall sheer into the water in curtains of various greys. The lake itself – the deepest in England – has a definite blue-green hue where it reflects the dark mountain. Nearby through the clear water I could see the rock slabs continuing until they disappeared into the green depths. As it is so near the sea, gulls are nearly always flying over its surface.

As most of this painting consists of rock, for which I mixed burnt sienna and ultramarine in varying proportions, the interest centred very greatly upon the rock forms, for which the tone values were of the greatest importance in suggesting sunlight.

All along this north-western shore there are many bays and rocky headlands. The granophyre outcrops by the lake have been the cause of some of the bays being graced by shores of palest pink shingle, and the mosses and brackens bring a richness of colour to the wildest lake in England.

Chapter 6

Loss

Although I had painted and drawn while in Sussex, my work had been spasmodic, so now I wanted to try to make up for the three years of the R.A. Schools that I had forgone. My R.A. school friend from Cumbria, Pat Millard, lived with his parents in Brixton where Canon Millard had his parish. Pat made me a very generous offer. He rented one of the Chenil studios, next to Chelsea Town Hall in King's Road, and he invited me to live in it if I would share the rent. It was a splendid studio, twenty feet square, with a gallery in which I slept. Here we were able to paint all daylight hours, hire models for drawing and entertain our friends and patrons.

I painted a good deal from studies made at home, in France and in Sussex. At that time the 'Studio' magazine introduced me to several patrons. I held my first London one man show in the Greenstone Gallery off Kings Road and sold fourteen paintings. I also showed at the R.A., the Royal Society of British Artists and the Goupil Gallery, and the Leicester Gallery, then one of the most important, promised me a show when I had got together a body of work. London Underground commissioned a poster, and I was asked to paint a mural in a country mansion in Surrey.

The winter of 1929 was the most severe for many years and an epidemic of influenza swept the country, claiming hundreds of lives. I became a victim, but, instead of accepting an invitation to Pat Millard's home, I tried to go on working in the studio.

Tophet Bastion, Gable (1937)

Boat People, Buenos Aires (1931)

On Saturday, with Pat at his home for the weekend, I was lying in bed feeling rather ill when there came a knock at the door. I just managed to climb down the ladder and open the door and then fainted. The visitors were Vera and Dennis, who had decided to come and see me as I would not go to see them. They got me off at once to St Luke's Hospital in Sidney Street, where I was found to have double pneumonia and pleurisy. The surgeon cut away part of a rib and drained the pus from the lungs by a rubber tube.

The dreams of delirium are as vivid now as are many memories of reality. It must have been at the time of the crisis that I imagined that I was up on the southern ridge above Borrowdale, looking down into a darkly wooded valley at the time just before sunrise, which was an event of the greatest importance and joy, but first I had to go down into the valley by a narrow rocky path.

On this occasion, in reality, a lovely girl named April Adams was sitting beside me, as she did every evening after her work as a model. I was partly aware of her presence and very concerned how she was going to get down the path in the dainty city shoes I knew she wore.

I firmly believe that this imaginary problem saved me from dying that night. Ever since this experience I have had no fear of death, and I am quite sure that it can be a glorious happening.

All the time I was in hospital Pat Millard climbed up seven flights of stairs every evening to see me, and the worried expression on his usually cheerful face would always make me laugh. My father came to London to see me for a few days, but he was looking unusually thin and ill and soon returned home. The influenza epidemic had taken toll of the hospital staff and they were very short handed. One day Pat, and a friend, Adrian Hill, brought me a sketch pad and some conté chalks, so I was fairly happy for another month. Then the hospital authorities suspected tuberculosis and I was sent to the Royal Sea Bathing Hospital at Margate. I had to stay there three months, but no tuberculosis was found.

While I was still at the hospital I heard that my father was dying of cancer. The hospital kindly discharged me and I arrived a few hours after my father had passed away on July 21st, 1929, at the age of 66.

I was too ill to attend the funeral, but my mother and my sister Una coped bravely with the situation and I believe the responsibility helped them in their grief.

A rough slab of green slate marked the final resting place of my father's body, in the churchyard of St Mary's Ambleside, but his real memorial is in the hearts of his loved ones, in his simple integrity and sunny character, and in the hundreds of vigorous landscapes he left behind all over the world.

Fairfield Range from Graithwaite. (1952)

LANGSTRATH BECK (1962)

A few hundred yards upstream from its junction with Greenup Beck the waters of Langstrath tumble, glide, slither and foam over the series of steps carved out of the hard Borrowdale volcanic rock – the hardest slate in the world – by the action of water, first in the form of ice and now as powerful torrents of water. The glaciers produced the flowing curves on the top of each strata, laid in skins of fairly even thickness of cooling volcanic lava, then pressed for thousands of years beneath the oceans. After the ice had gone, the tremendous and persistent power of running water has plucked great chunks from each skin of rock, forming the vertical cleavage. Here we see in one glance most of the make-up and the carving of the fells. For this subject an elementary knowledge of geology helps a good deal in interpreting visually one of the most interesting streamscapes that I know. The forms at first appear impossibly complex until one can realise something of how it all happened. Then one can select all that reveals this "happening", leaving out all that doesn't.

The many variations of green and blue-greys of the rocks, smoothed and scoured by centuries of floods, is varied where it is half-revealed, as through a veil of shallow gliding water, and darker and richer in the green or umber darks into which some light is reflected from the white foam.

Having understood with my mind, it required a certain amount of "brio" to put it all down in clear direct washes that might suggest the always fascinating interplay between the static and the moving, the permanent and the fleeting, each affecting the other though at very different paces.

Chapter 7

Climbs

The house, Cross Bow, which my father had bought from the poet, Sir William Watson, was still with much of the mortgage to pay, so my mother and sister held a special memorial exhibition of my father's work in his Norwegian studio in Lake Road, and this helped to pay some of the debts. Meanwhile, my doctor told us that I would not survive another winter unless I spent it in a sunny climate.

One Wednesday, Mrs Edith MacIver, a friend of our family came to tea. Her husband had owned a small shipping line that ran cargo ships between Liverpool and Buenos Aires. She asked me if I would care to go as supercargo on the SS Burgundy from Liverpool on the following Saturday, so I was delighted to accept such a wonderful offer.

The Burgundy weighed 2500 tons. She was thirty years old and this was her last voyage. One December 8th, when we were due to sail, a mighty storm was raging, so no ships, not even the big Cunarders, were able to leave Liverpool for another two days. When we sailed the seas were still too rough to drop the pilot, so we landed him in Lynas Bay, Anglesey, where we anchored for the night.

During the next few days of the storm several hundred barrels of kerosene, that had been lashed together on the open well deck close to the exposed steering gear, broke loose, and all hands turned out to chase them as they crashed across the deck which, every few mintues, was deluged by enormous seas. It was a wonder no one was washed overboard.

During the slow voyage down the South Atlantic I recovered my health steadily. I spent the time making sketches on board ship, and the captain allowed me to paint the names on the lifeboats and even to take the dog watch at the wheel. One of the paintings I did on board the Burgundy was purchased later by Lord Howard de Walden who told me it reminded him of his own days at sea; another by Sam Courtauld, the art dealer and great benefactor to the arts. Another painting, one reproduced in 'The Studio', was bought by Lady Sophie Gray, who lived in a large house with walled gardens in Trafalgar Square, Chelsea.

While I was in Buenos Aires I stayed with Mr and Mrs Udny Atkinson on their ranch a few miles from the city. They introduced me to several members of the British colony in Buenos Aires, who told me that, even as early as 1930, the German colony had been rapidly increasing.

I painted mostly in the dockland area of the city, especially around the Boca, the old port that was jammed tight with small native boats, many of them being used as living quarters. People would often stop and talk to me while I was painting, and one Norwegian seaman, when I rashly told him that I was half Norwegian, took me to see a compatriot of his who was suffering from tuberculosis on board an American cargo ship. Without any hesitation they took

Aconcagua, Argentina (1931)

my advice that he should be taken to hospital in Buenos Aires instead of waiting until they arrived in New York.

Mr Atkinson managed the Central Argentine Railway and he arranged for me a journey across Argentina to Puente del Inca, a small wooden hotel some 10,000 feet up, close to the Chilean border, to a natural bridge across the Rio Mendoza, and to Aconcagua, at 23,038 feet the highest mountain in the southern hemisphere and in both Americas. The imperfect state of my lungs and the fairly sudden change in altitude and temperature from the heat of Buenos Aires made my breathing rather difficult at first, but I soon became acclimatised.

Here I painted and roamed around, reaching 14,000 feet up the side of Aconcagua and narrowly missing encounters with Chilean smugglers. I wanted very much to look across the border into Chile, but, being a member of the crew of the Burgundy, I had a passport only for Argentina. I heard about a narrow track across the Andean Ridge, named appropriately 'Paso de los Contrabandistos', as it was used mainly by smugglers.

I started up the track until I saw, coming to meet me, a powerful Chilean. Hurriedly moving above the track I pretended to be making a drawing in my sketch book, with one eye on the Chilean, who, to my relief, as soon as he had passed below me, started to run until he disappeared from sight behind a bluff.

One day I attempted to traverse a buttress above the Rio Mendoza in order to paint Aconcagua from a higher level. The rock was very brittle and gave way under my feet when half way across. I dropped my easel which disappeared over a precipice so I had to retreat. On the following day a young Argentine engineer kindly came with me to try to recover the easel. On the way to the buttress I noticed traces of oil in the earth, which greatly interested my Argentine friend. We searched the buttress for my easel, without success, descending on the far side. By this time I was too weak to return over the buttress, so the only alternative was to cross the turbulent river and walk home along the railway line. The water was of an opaque red colour and I found the crossing, without ice axe or other support, quite difficult in the strong current.

There were several avalanche tunnels to negotiate and, just inside them, groups of Chilean workmen asleep in their blankets. My friend kept twirling his

Rio Mendoza, Argentina (1931)

Foot of Gimmer Crag, Langdale (1933)

ice axe rather nervously, and he explained on our return, that Chilean workmen had a nasty habit of robbing and murdering lone travellers.

I rejoined the Burgundy at Rosario, 200 miles up the Rio de la Plata, and had a delightfully sunny journey home, lying often in swim suit on the open well deck and being washed by occassional waves. There is no doubt that the five month journey saved my life once again.

One day in 1923, June Archer, a grand-daughter of Mrs MacIver, came with a friend, Major Gordon Osmaston, and asked me to take them rock climbing, assuming that I had had some experience. Actually I had never been on a climbing rope, as my parents had strictly forbidden it, though I had done a great deal of scrambling on rocks alone – much more dangerous.

I had heard of Gimmer Crag in Langdale from Jonathan Stables, a pioneer of routes on the Crag, notably of Amen Corner. I borrowed forty feet of cart rope from a farmer, and eventually we found the crag. An easy ledge, Ash Tree Ledge, ran diagonally halfway up the crag, so we took it as far as it went, some 150 feet above the base, then started climbing up from there. I was leading, and came to an overhang which I failed to negotiate, so I returned to the tiny pulpit where my friends were waiting. Gordon then had a try with the same result but he couldn't get down. June sat on my legs while I hung out over space and fielded Gordon on to the pulpit as he jumped.

We did actually achieve a climb, Chimney Buttress, on a crag that contains no climb below 'severe', then hurried over to Pavey Ark and climbed Rake End Chimney, which seemed quite easy after the exposure of Gimmer. Years later we learned that the climb we failed on was first climbed in 1948, named Kipling Groove and rated as 'very severe'. Needless to say this was just about the worst way to start rock climbing.

Gordon and June married soon afterwards. They are among my best friends and live in Grasmere where we see each other almost every day.

Gordon has served most of his adult life in the Royal Engineers entirely on survey work a good deal of it in the Himalayas, retiring with the rank of brigadier. While Shipton and Tilman were climbing Nanda Devi, at 25,645 feet the highest mountain in what was then the British Empire, Gordon and his team of Sherpas ascended the Rishi Ganga Gorge and surveyed around the inner sanctuary. The name of one of the Sherpas was Tensing Norkay. It was his first experience as a porter, and, on the way down, he fell ill. Gordon shared his tent with him and carried him part of the way down on his back. In his book 'Man of Everest', translated by James Ullman, Tensing wrote about this as first contact with an Englishman. He is now the director of a mountaineering school at Darjeeling, and he met Gordon again while he was staying with Lord Hunt at his home near Henley-on-Thames.

Not knowing any other climbers at that time, I found I had to lead most of the climbs I did with odd strangers I met while on painting expeditions at Burnthwaite and the hotel at Wasdale Head and elsewhere. It was not until I joined the Fell and Rock Climbing Club of the English Lake District, (to give it its full title for once), that I learned what it was to climb with good climbers such as Ernest Wood-Johnson, A. B. Hargreaves, Colin Kirkus, A. T. and Ruth Hargreaves, C. F. Holland, G. R. Speaker, J. H. Doughty, Astley Cooper, Bill Hennessy, Sid Cross, Mabel Barker, Alf Bridge, Jack Longland, H. M. Kelly, Blanche Eden-Smith, J. H. B. Bell, Tony Musgrave, Nancy Ridyard, Dick Cook, Bentley Beetham, Howard and Leslie Somervell, R. S. T. Chorley, John Appleyard, Alan Austin, Jack Soper and John Hunt, on a variety of much more interesting climbs.

One of the most delightful of climbing days I had was on Dow Crag. I had mentioned to Tony Musgrave that, looking from C Buttress, I could hardly believe that the overhang on "Eliminate A" was possible, so he and Nancy Ridyard took me up it. As it was a gloriously hot day in September, I first had a dip in the Brathay just below Skelwith Force, then we all had another, after the enjoyable climb, in Goats Water, diving into the clear water from the great boulders of the scree, and yet another in Torver Beck, to end a very enjoyable day.

On the occasion of an Easter meet, I was leading a social trio up Blizzard Chimney when I heard the unmistakable sound of someone falling. I handed over the lead to G. Eden-Smith and, on descending to the bed of Easter Gully, I

Evening, Pillar (1934)

saw a man dangling from the second pitch of Hopkinson's Crack and a young boy holding him on the rope from a ledge above. I managed to brace my leg across the crack and take the strain of the semi-concious man off the rope, to the relief of the boy, who had burnt his hands while trying to check the fall. Several of us lowered the man down to the foot of the crag by suspending him from a spider's web of ropes. We had to wait five cold hours for a doctor and stretcher to arrive from Coniston.

An incident of a happier kind comes to mind. I was walking along the High Level Route to Pillar with Kelly and Holland, at that time two giants of the world of British rock climbing, when, without a word, both men swerved to the right off the track, walked a few feet down the slope and stopped in front of a spring of crystal clear water that came bubbling out of cushions of moss, out of which grew the most lovely young shoots of a saxifrage. The three of us stood around it in silence for a few minutes, then continued on our way.

In 1933 I joined a New Year climbing party at the Royal Oak Hotel, Borrowdale, composed of Jack and Mrs Longland, Paul and Mrs Sinker, Ashley and Mrs Miles, Biddy Chew and several others, adding up to a dozen. On New Year's Day we all set off to climb on Scafell. On our arrival at Hollow Stones it was agreed that Jack Longland should lead one half of the party and I the other. My six had an enjoyable climb up Moss Ghyll, returning to Hollow Stones as darkness was setting in. Some time later Jack's party arrived in pitch darkness, and had some difficulty in finding their rucksacks among the many boulders. The only light we had among us was my small pocket torch which I swung at regular intervals along the twelve of us as we trudged in heavy rain along the Corridor Route. At one point I flashed the torch back to find Paul Sinker waist-deep in a small tarn, still holding aloft a candle lantern that he had been trying in vain to light.

Another good friend whom I met through climbing was Jim Cameron. I was staying at Blacksail Hut, the Youth Hostel Centre at the head of Ennerdale, while making some drawings of Pillar Rock for a rock climbing guide book. One evening two men got talking to me and told me they had never done any rock

Y Garn from Tryfan, Wales (1937)

climbing and would I take them on the following day to the Pillar? I said I would take them on a climb after finishing the drawings. As it turned out I took them up six climbs, starting with a moderate climb, Slab and Notch, and finishing with the North climb 'a hard difficult' with one 'severe' pitch, the Nose. Jim Cameron was second on the rope and came up without much difficulty, but the third man, a journalist on the 'Yorkshire Post', almost fainted and had to be hauled over the Nose. Jim accompanied me on my homeward journey and we did several climbs en route on Great Gable, including Napes Needle, which excited Jim so much that he wanted to stand on his head on the tiny summit, but forgot in the excitement of getting there.

Jim was trained at Barrow-in-Furness as a boiler maker, but was working at that time in a hotel in Llandudno. He became so keen that he used to cycle the 155 miles to Grasmere on Friday nights, climb with me on Saturday and Sunday and return on Sunday night. At first I used to take it for granted that I would lead the climbs, until over New Year in 1937, I rented the Youth Hostel at Blacksail, at the head of Ennerdale, (which was normally closed during the winter) for a fortnight, asking H. M. Kelly and J. M. Doughty, both famous in the climbing world, to join Jim and myself for the last week.

On one wet day before they arrived I thought we might try working out a route on Raven Crag, below Pillar Rock, so that, by linking it up with the North West climb, one could get over 700 feet of climbing. As the angle looked fairly easy, I asked Jim if he would care to lead. The slope was rather deceptive and Jim led a severe climb of 340 feet which we named Centipede.

A few years later, after he had had some narrow escapes from death with me and other climbers, Jim gave up his job and set up as a professional mountain guide, soon building up a good clientèle for climbs in Scotland and the Alps as well as in the Lake District. He went on to become a member of the Fell and Rock Climbing Club, a founder member of the Coniston Mountain Rescue Squad and president of the Lancashire Caving and Climbing Club.

One of his greatest and most successful adventures was marrying his wife Betty. It was in the second year of the war, and Jim was back in his old job as boiler maker in Barrow-in-Furness. Betty Ivens had been one of his climbing clients. Her relatives were members of the aristocracy, and the wedding was held at a London church.

Jim bought a suit, packed it in his suitcase and set off for London. On Preston station, where he changed trains, he met a climbing friend, Dick Cook, so the result was that his train departed without him, but with his suitcase. Betty gallantly kept her family at the church for an hour and a half until Jim arrived, running, in his working clothes, but I gather that all went well from that point!

Some months later, in the middle of a very wet summer, Jim invited Betty's mother to stay with them at an isolated, and then rather primitive, farm at Seathwaite in Borrowdale, distinguished for having the heaviest rainfall in England. Contrary to our fears it was a great success. Mrs Ivens so fell for Jim that, in her later years, she came to live with them, together with her husband.

By this time Jim's two sons, Alistair, (whose godfather I am), and Hugh, had begun to make their way in the world.

They all had a very happy and active life together until one day, in April 1981, Jim, after mowing the lawn, sat down in a chair and passed peacefully away.

Jim Cameron (1979)

Scafell from Beckhead Winter (1934)

BLEA TARN, NOVEMBER 1982

This slight hollow between the two Langdales was scooped out by the overspill of the glacier that flowed down Great Langdale from the central fells around Scafell.

The day of painting was in early November, after the first snows of winter had fallen and had time to thaw from the rock faces, leaving a lacy filigree of white in the gullies.

I chose to paint from the Lingmoor shore of the tarn, for, from here, one can enjoy the curve of the margin, so much more interesting a shape than the horizontal far edge as seen from the usual view. From here, too, a rib of rock descends to the tarn from the grassy slopes, and a few boulders enliven the foreground.

I started with the sky, slow-moving clouds beyond the Pikes. The latter I painted in permutations of cobalt blue mixed with light red for the rocky formations, bluer towards Pike of Stickle and warmer for Harrison Stickle, gradually adding more light red for the lower slopes of grass and bracken. In these colours, with burnt sienna and yellow ochre added, I painted the rocky profile of Side Pike on the right and, darker, the slopes from Blake Rigg on the left.

The climax of colour came in the flatter ground between the col and the tarn, and here I let myself go with full-brush swathes of yellow ochre, raw sienna and burnt sienna, and cadmium yellow in the narrow band of rushes by the tarn. There was a hint of warm green in the immediate foreground.

It was a still, mild day, and, apart from a breeze far away that reflected the sky, all the mountains were reflected in the tarn, those of the snow-streaked Pikes mingling with the rounded glacial boulders in the foreground.

So I was able to start and finish this painting out-of-doors on site, always a most satisfying and educative exercise.

Chapter 8

Decision

By the year 1931 we were living in a rented house at White Bridge, Grasmere. This meant that, if the studio in Ambleside was to be open, I had to cycle the four miles from Grasmere and spend the day there, as no one else in the family would help. The result was that either I was in the studio trying to sell pictures while, all the time, longing to be out painting them, or, when I was out painting, I was worried for much of the time about the studio being closed.

After a few years of this I was in a rather desperate state of frustration. I managed to get in some painting and climbing occasionally, but, all the time, a powerful resentment against my mother and my sister Una was growing inside me. I felt rather like a mouse on a treadmill, and I could not see how I would ever be able to lead a life of my own, get married and have a family. I was naturally attracted to girls, and I slept around with several who were aware of what they were doing, but I think I must have been a bitter man at that time. I felt that I was gradually prostituting any ability for serious painting, all my dreams of becoming a good painter, in order to earn enough to support four people, the fourth being my delightful deaf Norwegian Aunt Otalia, who lived in a cottage in Langdale. This situation, I argued, in a way justified my own indulgencies in relationships with several women for whom I had little, if any, love.

We had not been able to earn enough money through selling my father's and my work, although I still exhibited in the Royal Academy and other mixed shows, so I decided to spend four of the winter months in London, making as much money as quickly as possible and then coming home and trying to do seriously good work.

When I got to London I made a list from the trades directory of several theatrical scene painters. The first one I visited was Edward Delany, whose studios were in Cricklewood. He asked to see some of my work, which I brought the same day. Delany said he would 'phone' me if anything turned up. The next day he 'phoned to ask me to go to the studios. There he showed me a canvas backcloth 60 feet by 30 feet, lying on the floor, and a great many chamber pots containing powder colours and size, and he told me to paint a landscape in the style of Dutch tiles. I went off with a sketch pad to the Victoria and Albert Museum and made many drawings, brought them back and started to design, all of which had taken three or four days.

Then Delany came and told me that I was too slow – his own men could have finished it in two days. So he put me on to designing and painting first small special features, gradually entrusting me to carrying out the decor for whole scenes. Edward and his two brothers were Austrian-Irish, and Edward, the head of the firm, had studied art in Vienna and could paint in a vigorous Austrian style. Sometimes a job would come in that had been designed by some well-known artist who had little knowledge of the stage, so we translated his slight sketches into three dimensions, usually by making a scale model out of cardboard. One of these productions was the famous review 'White Horse Inn'. It was in the early days of the revolving stage, so this new development, installed at Covent Garden Theatre, gave us plenty of scope for invention.

The continental method of scene painting is to lay the canvas on the floor, walking over it with padded shoes, and viewing it from a tall step ladder or a gallery, while the British method is to hang it vertically on a frame that can be raised by pulleys, the whole of a normally large backcloth moving between two floors.

At that time theatres were demanding sets made from such fragile materials as tin foil and velvet, which could not be hung, so Delany's were very much in demand. Edward, I found, was a very good employer. He paid me double when one of my sets pleased his client, and, at the end of the winter, he said that I could come back to him at any time for as long or as short as I liked. If he had no work for me himself he introduced me to film art directors and to firms engaged in interior decoration of large buildings, so, during the winter months of the next three years, I had an interesting time designing for films, and for interior decoration of buildings in Picadilly and Oxford Street, working for such people as the Korda brothers, Michael Powell and Marc Henri Laverdet.

But I found that I could not keep the two halves of myself separate, so, after a few years, I gave up London and painted my own work throughout the year.

One day early in 1934 I had a visit from the two eminent climbers, H. M. Kelly

In a Film Studio (1936)

Harry Kelly (1937)

Kelly on North Wall, Pillar (1937)

and B. Eden Smith. Harry Kelly had just been appointed to the position of the editor of the climbing guides to the district.

The first guide in the next series was to be one of Pillar Rock, Ennerdale. Earlier guides had been illustrated by photographs, which did not always show whether a dark patch, for instance, was an overhang or a bunch of heather, and, also, had the disadvantage of showing equally every detail on the crag.

They asked me if I would try some drawings that showed the structure of the crag, but also showed any feature that was relevant to the climb. I find, in Harry's meticulously complete diary, that the first meeting of the Guide Committee was held on June 3rd, 1933. So the next day off we went to Ella Naylor's farm, Middle Row at Wasdale Head, and then began a series of highly enjoyable journeys up by Blacksail Pass and Looking Stead and the High Level Route to Pillar. It was a good summer for weather, and I gradually invented an idiom which would fulfil the need. The drawings were reproduced in half-tone and the dotted lines, figures and letters of the routes in blacker letterpress.

Of course this meant that I was able to take part with Kelly and Holland and many of the best climbers in climbing severe routes on all the crags in the district over the years, which produced a new guide every few years as new routes were opened up. I shall never forget the occasion when Harry Kelly, Blanche Eden-Smith and I reached the foot of D climb on Gimmer, rated then as 'very severe' and they said to me 'You lead'.

Several of my friends went in awe of Harry on account of his usually fierce expression, his uptwirled moustache and his impatience with small talk. Over the many years of our association I found in him a delightful companion and one who was always at his best when things were difficult. He took an impish delight in shocking people. I remember arriving at the top of Windy Gap once when the beauty of the view and the day were almost breathtaking. When Harry joined me his remark was – 'Vury nice. I wish I were in Blackpool.'

He was very interested, of course, in my drawings of the crags, but also in drawing and painting for their own sakes, and I found that I could paint happily in his company. He took to painting later in life, and this, together with listening to good music and watching cricket, became the main interests of his later years.

Blanche Eden-Smith, known to her friends as G. (standing for the angel Gabriel, as she patiently recorded all our climbs), was almost the entire opposite of Harry. She was always steady and patient in her caring for people, and made the perfect encouraging second on a rope. She was a great friend of Harry's first wife, Pat, and, when Pat was killed while descending Tryfan, G. helped him through a dark period of his life and stood by him steadily over the years.

She was a founder member of the Pinnacle Club, which was composed of women climbers and had its headquarters in Wales. Her son, Waddy, inherited

Scafell Crag (1936)

his mother's love of climbing, and he and I had some enjoyable days on the fells, doing some first ascents in Deepdale. He joined the Navy at the beginning of the war and lost his life in the first year.

When I was illustrating the guide to Scafell, I found that the face of Scafell is best revealed in sunlit detail between five and six in the morning and about eight in the evening during the month of June. The structure of the crag is best seen in the morning, so that, when I needed a wash drawing of the whole face for the frontispiece of the Scafell Guide, I invited a young friend, Graham Hayes, to bivouac with me on top of Scafell Pike. While I was drawing, Graham explored the crag from Lord's Rake. After breakfast we were about to climb Moss Ghyll when two men came and told us they had found the body of a man in Deep Ghyll, and they asked if we would help when a stretcher had arrived from Wasdale Head. We agreed to join them when we had finished our climb. The dead man had been with a party on Scafell but had refused to descend with the others down Deep Ghyll, preferring to find his own way down Professor's Chimney, where the rock is rotten and dangerous. He was wearing boots with smooth leather soles and could hardly have been more accident prone.

Graham and I did several climbs together while he was making fine furniture at Temple Sowerby. In 1939 he joined the army, was soon transferred to Lord Lovat's newly formed regiment of commandos and, after taking part in a daring raid on St Nazaire, was caught and shot in spite of being a military prisoner.

I have always enjoyed finding interesting routes on some insignificant bit of rock that no one had bothered about, and it never occurred to me to record them, but just enjoy them. One of these was Lining Crag, on the right near the top of Greenup Gill in Borrowdale. I climbed a route solo one evening and, with Jim Cameron and later, with John Hunt, we did a few more and better ones. Now, the crag can provide eight routes, among them several 'severes' and a 'very severe'.

Another of these was Eagle Crag in Grisedale. On a sunny still morning in June 1937 I took my niece, Sheila, and a fourteen year old boy, Michael Rucklidge, over by Grisedale Tarn to Eagle Crag, on the west side of the valley

With A. B. Hargreaves on Pillar (1937)

Gordon and Craig Route, Dow Crag (1936)

about half way down to Patterdale. We collected a hound pup at Knott House Farm and he was quite content to lie at the foot of the crag while we explored three fairly easy routes. We all had a dip in the beck, and carried the weary pup home to the farm as the evening shadows were creeping up the fellsides. I see in the guide that there are nine routes now on the crag, including two 'very severes'.

Around about the early 1930s I initiated among my friends a phase of gill climbing, perhaps a kind of throw-back to the Stock Gill Club of my schooldays at Ambleside.

It started with one day before Easter when Jim Cameron and I were on the way to climb on Scafell from Langdale by way of the lovely strath of Upper Eskdale. The waterfall that runs from between Scafell Pike and Scafell, named, in true Cumbrian, Cam Spout, is really a series of short falls interspersed with crystal clear rock pools, extending over several hundred feet in all. We looked at each other and, without a word stripped off and climbed on plentiful holds up the dashing cascades, plunging into each pool on the way. It was a most exhilarating game, of which the only (unwritten and unspoken) rule was that one should climb in the water all the way.

Of course we extended this game to such places as Sourmilk Gill, Easdale; Hell Gill below Bowfell and Mill Gill that falls from Stickle Tarn.

Some months before D Day in the second world war, I was asked to take parties of army men on moderate rock climbs. One of our venues was on the gabbro Crags of Carrock Fell, ending usually with a visit to the extensive iron-age fort on the summit. Gabbro, the rock of the Skye Cuillin and, on Carrock, its only appearance in England, is much rougher and more crystalline in texture, more suited to the cheap rubber plimsolls supplied by the Army.

One day an officer and some 'ranks' wanted to climb on Pavey Ark. It was a broiling hot day in August so, instead of walking up beside Mill Gill, (or Stickle Gill as I prefer to call it) I climbed up in the water, and this immediately caught on with the troops. They behaved like a bunch of children, laughing and shouting all the way, but this became uproarious as we climbed up Little Gully on Pavey Ark, after some days of rain almost a waterfall.

Running or gliding water is always more exhilarating than when it's still, and dips in such rock pools as exist on the Esk and Langstrath Beck – always including Blackmoor Pot – both quite the most interesting mountain streams in England – were part of a day's climbing, as well as longer swims in the much colder tarns. Fortunately there were not so many people on the fells in those days to see our unadorned skins.

The delightful task of drawing for the guides continued for well over thirty years, and, quite undeservedly, the Club elected me an Honorary Member by way of thanks. For me the days on the rocks with Kelly and our friends were sheer delight.

One day later in 1934 Gordon and June Osmaston came and told me that they had both made the experiment of giving the whole of their lives for ever to God, and that they had found a new life together.

This happened in Oxford where they had met several people, known then as the Oxford Group, who were living this way, and living very effectively. As soon as they started to tell me, I knew subconsciously that this was what I needed to do myself. I had often trusted my life to these two during the many enjoyable rock climbs we had shared, and so I trusted them now. They told me a lot about themselves and I told them of my situation, leaving nothing out.

The next morning Gordon called and shared with me some thoughts he had had earlier in a time of quiet listening to God. He told me that there was a weekend gathering at an hotel near Kendal, and we agreed to go.

Meanwhile I had been doing some thinking of my own. I faced the fact that my life was far from satisfactory, because of my frustration and lack of love for my mother and sister, and for almost any of the women in my life. In fact I was just not capable of real love. I knew that I was a failure, even as a painter, and I was longing to hand over the control of my life to a God who I was no longer sure existed. I made one condition. I could not possibly give up painting even if God wanted me to, and of course, He wouldn't do that, otherwise what would we all live on?

All this was happening as I was alone on the second night after Gordon's sharing, and I knew, without anyone telling me, that the decision would have to

The Silent Quarry, Little Langdale (1954)

On Sty Head (1936)

be all or nothing. After hours of wrestling with all this, I knelt down and said, 'Alright God, I am ready to stop painting for ever if that's what you want'. Immediately it was as though a great weight had been lifted off me. I was intensely aware at that moment of the rain that was streaming down the mountains and blessing the valleys. I was aware of the presence and power and love of Christ.

Later when I read the 104th Psalm I realised that its writer had had a similar experience and sung about it in glorious word pictures.

The next morning Gordon came, we were quiet together, and wrote down our thoughts and shared them. I told him about my experience, and my further thought that morning was to tell my mother that I had been dishonest with her over money, allowing her to think that I shared all the income while I kept back certain sums for my own pleasure. She astonished me by saying that she had known this for a long time but she could not understand why I had told her now. So I told her what had happened to me, and, a few weeks later, she asked if she could live the same way.

On the Sunday following my release I went to church with Gordon, and the two words of Jesus Christ that came alive for me were:– 'If ye continue in my word, then are ye my disciples indeed. Ye shall know the truth and the truth shall make you free'. I had always wanted truth, and always wanted freedom. The other words which gave me great assurance were:– 'I am the vine and ye are the branches'. Thus at long last, came my experience of the redeeming love of Christ.

Gordon and I met each morning, and, at each time of waiting, I had thoughts about honesty which involved a great deal of restitution. One great help in this new life was to accept a sort of yardstick by which to measure oneself – absolute honesty, absolute purity, absolute unselfishness and absolute love. For me this showed me not only that I was a failure by absolute standards – Christ's standards – but precisely where and what to do about it now. And most surprising of all came the strength to put things right in my life, and the discovery that life became an exciting and enjoyable adventure.

For some five or six weeks I was fully occupied in the putting right of wrong relationships. My mother started life again at the age of 70. I found that Frithjof, my elder brother, had always been jealous of me, and he started life again as I had done. My sister, Una, almost came to the point but then retreated, and, sadly, had many and great difficulties later in her life.

One morning I had a clear thought to go and paint in a certain place at a certain time, which I gladly obeyed. This kind of thought kept recurring, and I realised that God had given me back my gift of painting to be used in His service. Over the years, painting had become my real security instead of God.

Building The Studio, Grasmere (1938)

Gradually people began to see a new quality in my work, and also in me. I found that other people wanted what I had been given, among them a young communist teacher, although I had done nothing to try to influence them. Gradually, through working with others who were living this way, I began to see that the whole world was meant to be governed by people governed by God, that this was the real intention behind the creation of Man.

At this time I was very curious to know more about the work of the Oxford Group. I heard there was to be a conference in Oxford that summer, so I bought a ten-year-old Austin Seven car for £6 and invited Jim Cameron to come and camp with me near Oxford to attend some of the meetings. Neither of us could drive a car, so I learnt on the way, without any mishaps.

I was keen to meet Dr Frank Buchman, through whom the Oxford Group movement came into being in 1921, and to tell him that, instead of 'changing' university types, he should go for the really 'important people', artists and communists. I managed to waylay him in the garden of Lady Margaret Hall and, as we walked around, I got off my chest all that I was thinking. The only words he said to me were 'That's fine, Heaton. Go ahead', and he left me to think.

During the summer of 1938, this great pioneer and Christian, Frank Buchman, called with two young men to see me in Grasmere. After lunch with my mother and myself, he asked me to come with him and his friends, Michael Barrett and Arthur Strong, to Keswick to see the small chapel in which he had had an experience of Christ in 1908. That experience was the beginning of the movement which over the years, became the Oxford Group and of the philosophy which, in 1938, entered the world under the name of Moral Rearmament.

Both my mother and I were convinced that I should build a good stone house, studio and a gallery, in the middle of Grasmere. At that time my credit at the bank was £120. However, the thought persisted and, by degrees, each practical step was revealed. The first one was to write a large, well-illustrated book which I called 'The Hills of Lakeland'. I had never written anything but short articles before, but the book was written and all fifty-two paintings to illustrate it were done during 1937. Frederick Warnes published it in a handsome form, with 250 larger de-luxe autographed volumes, and it sold well from the start, with quite good press reviews.

After being led to buying a small plot of land adjoining the village green, the very place I had in mind, the book helped me to sell enough paintings to pay for a building society to start work, and, as soon as they had finished the gallery, I quickly hung up paintings on the walls and sold them in order to keep the men at work completing the next part of the building. The whole work was completed within 1938. All the time I never had any fears or doubts about the outcome.

Rydal Oak (1955)

HAZY MORNING, CRUMMOCK WATER (1956)

This is the place I enjoy more than anywhere else in the world.

Whenever I walk down the rounded grassy flanks of Melbreak to the curved bay by the ancient pele peninsula, along the light vari-coloured shore made of flat Skiddaw slate pebbles, perfect for ducks and drakes, with, here and there, a pink granite boulder that has fallen from one of the metamorphic fells between here and Red Pike, or a smoother green slab of rock brought down by glacial action from the head of the valley, I seem to expand and to glow with pleasure in all that feeds my eyes and my spirit.

From here, the fells on each side of the lake descend in steep flowing curves that flatten out towards its margin. On the right, the heather slopes of Melbreak lead on to Red Pike, High Stile, High Crag and, last, Great Gable, seven miles away on the horizon.

On the left, the magnificent peak of Rannerdale Knott stands dramatically against the southern light, above the fields of Rannerdale farm.

Beside the natural composition of forms, the attraction that May morning was the light. Especially subtle were the delicate gradations of tones of the fells on the right, that became paler and bluer up the length of the valley.

To suggest the warm hazy sunlight – typical of the Lake District rather than of any other country – I flooded the whole paper, except the gleams of light far up the lake, starting very wet at the top with cobalt and vermilion, gradually reducing the blue towards the horizon, and, when I came to the sunlit foreground, painted it in the lightest tones of light red mixed with cadmium yellow. This all dried quickly in the sun, so then I started with Gable, in palest cobalt blue, gradually deepening and warming the shades of blue and grey, adding purples and siennas to the sunlit fellsides, ochres to the grasses, pale flicks of light red to suggest flat pebbles, greens and pinks of the boulders with their shadowed sides lit by reflected light, and, finally, the warm darks – burnt sienna and ultramarine – of the wall and railings.

The small accents of dark in the foreground accentuated the light in the painting, in spite of its quiet colours, and the gleams on the far end of the lake gave a tone to the blue fells.

Reflections were painted in horizontal strokes with a large brush, the water deepening in tone towards the foreground.

Rarely have I felt so at peace while painting out-of-doors from nature, and something of the feeling of the day and place has got into the painting.

Chapter 9

Marriage

One wet afternoon in 1938 an old friend from Ulverston days, Miss Dorothea Billinge, came into my Ambleside studio with her niece, Ophelia Gordon Bell. They had been walking in the rain and Ophelia's hair was streaming wet, and I knew at once that she was to be my companion for life.

I was engaged in planting trees and shrubs in the garden of the new studio in Grasmere when the day came for me to propose our marriage. I sent her an invitation, painted on a long scroll of somewhat Chinese proportions, inviting her to come and find some young wild birches and rowans up on the fellside and to help me to plant them. It was a blustery showery day in November, and I was entranced by everything about her, particularly by the loving way in which she patted the young trees into their new home. We went to see a film in Kendal and, on the way back, beside the road near the Windermere golf course, I asked her to marry me. My relief was almost overwhelming when she said 'Yes'.

Then began some wonderfully happy days on the fells, walking and painting and skating on the tarns. We learned much about each other, and I became more and more sure that we were meant for each other.

I find it rather difficult, now, for me to describe her, having been so close to her, so I must rely partly on the effect she had on other people. The first quality about her that struck me was her vitality, combined with an eagerness of spirit that wanted to experience the inner truth about people, places, relationships, and especially sculpture and paintings. Great music meant a very great deal to her. She was deeply devoted to her lovely mother and to her aunt Dorothea – Auntie Dolly – who had provided a second home, which she called her real home, for her during a great deal of her childhood. She made a few really deep friendships that lasted for life, and yet she gave out so much to everyone she met. The lady who has come one morning a week for years to help with the housework said to me today about Ophelia, 'She had a kind of aura. As soon as I set foot in the house, I could tell if she was in'.

Like every true artist, she carried through every work she took on with immense zest, and to its conclusion. She was physically very strong – one farmer

The Shadowed Farm, Troutbeck (1964)

Anthony Chapman, Huntsman (1967)

we passed in Cockermouth remarked about her, 'Strong as a horse' – and her temper, whenever it flared up, was devastating.

Ophelia lived for most of the year with her mother as paying guests in the home, in St Johns Wood, London, of another aunt, Muriel, who was the wife of Dr Caleb Saleeby, a celebrated pioneer in eugenics, clean air, sunlight and several branches of preventitive medicine. Ophelia's mother, Winifred, known to her family and friends as Tommy, was an extremely beautiful woman with dark brown hair and large deep-set eyes, more conventionally beautiful than Ophelia. She was a painter of animals, having been a student at Calderon's school in London, while Muriel, who was a very gifted pianist, was being trained at the Royal College of Music. Among their great friends were Sir Henry and Lady Wood, and Sir Adrian and Lady Boult. Keith Faulkner, who later became president of the Royal College of Music, was a dear friend of Ophelia – she always took him a box of ginger whenever she went to hear him sing – and she was constantly meeting musical people, including the BBC orchestra, in the house and at tennis parties.

The only schooling she ever had was for a year at King Alfred's School, Hampstead, and, a few earlier years, at a small private school, Oakburn, in Windermere. The rest of her education was by means of a governess, and one of the results was that her mathematics were almost unbelievably bad. Occasionally Dr Saleeby would take the whole family to Vevey, beside the Lake of Geneva, for several months of the summer, and, on one memorable occasion, they all spent a winter in Florence, driven there through the snow by their chauffeur in their large black Humber. So Ophelia enjoyed an interesting and unusual childhood, spending the summers with her aunt Dorothea in Windermere. For her, the Lake District had always been her real home.

When she was fifteen she became a student at the Regent Street Polytechnic School of Sculpture. This was the beginning of a new independence. She formed there several lifelong friendships and became a very talented sculptor under Professor Brownsword, Marjorie Crossley (later Osborne) and Geoffrey Deeley. By 1938 her sculpture had attracted some notice among the critics. She exhibited in the Royal Academy, the Glasgow Institute of Fine Arts, and the Royal Scottish Academy in Edinburgh, and she carried out several portrait commissions, as well as a bronze memorial plaque for a bridge in British Guiana.

Her mother used to receive commissions for paintings of horses and dogs and, beside a small annuity, they both had no money other than what they could earn, though they paid their share of expenses in the Saleeby household.

During 1939, with war clouds gathering ever more darkly in Europe, Ophelia began to have doubts about our marriage.

She was twenty four, immensely attractive to people of both sexes chiefly through her great vitality, her gift of friendship and her creative imagination that expressed itself in her sculpture and her love of great music and poetry. Her whole life and soul were in the embodiment of Christ's words. 'Blessed are they which do hunger and thirst after righteousness, for they shall be filled.' All life was before her and it was rich in promise.

I was already thirty five, with quite a lot of adventure and seeking behind me and a clear direction before me. I was definitely 'in love' with her body and her spirit, while she was never 'in love' with me, though her love for me grew and deepened during the year of our betrothal and throughout all our life together. Probably because of the failure of her parents' marriage, she had, in 1939, a deep fear of the commitment of marriage, and this fear had a tendency to recur occasionally in after years, especially when the challenge of the total commitment to Christ of other people caused her to look inwards.

During the summer of 1939 we spent a few days at Brackenclose, the Fell and Rock Climbers' hut at the head of Wastwater, climbing with Bill Stallybrass and Margot Bigland, both committed Christians and, like ourselves, engaged to be married. As Ophelia and I walked home down Langdale she told me fully and honestly about her doubts over our marriage.

It was the darkest day of my life. For over a year I had known that the right direction was a life with her, yet I felt sure it would not work out unless she too was sure. She wanted to postpone a decision, but it seemed clear to me that the only way was to make a clean break, to return each others' presents and not to communicate unless it was clearly right to do so. As far as I knew, we would

Shamrock, Pillar (1935)

The Road to Crummock Water (1952)

never see each other again. It seemed like committing suicide, and, for her too, it was a shattering blow.

When war was declared in September, Ophelia was immediately called up in the First Aid Nursing Yeomanry (FANY) with which she had been training for three years. She was made a corporal and was put in charge of nine women drivers and their vans, and based in Davyhulme Hospital, Manchester. Meanwhile I had been turned down as C3 by a medical board on account of my damaged lungs, and I applied to Air Ministry for a post as camouflage officer. While waiting for a reply I helped to form the Grasmere contingent of the Home Guard and was made sergeant in spite of my shocking performances at the rifle range. Quite out of the blue one morning I had the thought to send a telegram to Ophelia, whom I had not seen for a year, saying 'Will you marry me?' After a lot of heart searching she replied, 'Yes, in May'.

At that time anyone could leave the FANY Corps on marriage. A month after Ophelia resigned, this rule was cancelled when the Corps became part of the ATS (Auxilliary Territorial Service) though we did not know this at the time. So Ophelia and I were married quietly on the morning of May 25th, 1940, in St Oswald's Church, Grasmere.

We had both separately had the same idea for where to spend our honeymoon. It was at the Kirkstile Inn, Loweswater, at that time a farm as well as an inn, kept by the Stagg family. We camped along the western shore of Crummock Water under heather-clad Melbreak, eventually settling near the foot of Scale Beck, among bluebells and ancient hawthorn trees in full wedding bloom. The weather was glorious all the time. While I painted, Ophelia would return to the inn and telephone home to ask if the Home Guard needed us, but always the answer from Major Gordon was, "There's no need. You'll only have one honeymoon, so stay on". For a year or so Marianne Lederer, a Jewish

Dawn Over The Scafells (1981)

refugee from Czechoslovakia, had been living with us at the studio, and it was she who kept everything running in our absence.

Eventually, after ten sun-drenched days, we decided it was right to return home. By that time we had collected so much gear – tent, sleeping bags, painting kit and even a gramophone – that we could not possibly carry it for three miles back to the inn, so we made a raft out of our rubber inflatable mattresses, braced with some old railings and lashed together with climbing rope. This we pulled along the shore, swimming occasionally round rocky headlands such as Ling Point, the glaciated rock linked to Melbreak by a narrow strip of shingle.

We returned home in the midst of Home Guard activities. Our studio became the gathering point and store for rifles and uniforms. We were on guard in the old drill hall for 24 hours each day, each of the three platoons taking eight hour shifts. And at every red warning alert we really expected to deal with an invasion.

In July 1940 I was called up by Air Ministry for training as a camouflage officer. This took place in Bush House, Kingsway, London, where several other artists and architects were taking the same course, including Hugh Casson, now President of the Royal Academy. I had never flown before, and my first experience was in an unarmed Anson trainer at night above Kidlington near Oxford, while enemy bombers were over London. Some of the work was interesting, such as a spell of being flown at 2,000 feet over much of England, choosing sites for fuel storage tanks. It was interesting to observe the great variation in the colour of the soil in different counties.

Quiet apart from work, I was invited, together with a few men from other ministries, to fire-watch in Westminster Abbey. It was fascinating to walk along the high string galleries where one could see sculpture hardly visible from ground level. I enjoyed, too, climbing out on the roof, up and down cat ladders, and on to pinnacles high above Parliament Square. Every evening the Dean would come and visit us, carrying a lantern, which showed the fan vaulting of the King Henry VII chapel as it must have been seen when it was built.

After only a month's training I was sent for a week to the North West area to see the work in action. The camouflage officer, Ronald Dann, had been there since before the war, and was very helpful in taking me around and explaining everything. One morning a message came from Air Ministry, London, saying that I was to take over the area, and that Ronald Dann was to stay on as my assistant! The position was so ridiculous, but we had to obey orders, so we agreed that I should do the designing and flying and receive any knocks that might come, while Ron managed the work of the 400 men who were spread over all R.A.F. installations between Cheshire and Cumberland, including the Isle of Man.

Ennerdale in Spring (1980)

Family Carols. (1950)

The most successful work we did was to conceal nerve centres such as Fighter Command Controls and various radar installations, entirely covering such comparatively small targets with wire netting, painted to resemble fields or slag heaps. Anyway, not one of our camouflaged targets was bombed. I was glad to be able to introduce a few reforms, mainly to save the import of thousands of gallons of Bitumen with which to simulate hedgerows. I used real heather.

Eventually, in 1945, came peace, and with it all reunions, rejoicings and also the problems.

Apart from food shortages and the presence of many refugees, the war hardly touched the Lake District. My brother, Frithjof, had joined the RAF and was invalided home with wounds, which, in later years, caused his death. My mother had become almost immobilised with arthritis.

Ophelia had borne a daughter on February 19th, 1943, whom we called Otalia after my Norwegian aunt, and, on December 16th, 1944, our first son was born, whom we call John Christian.

Somehow, throughout the war years, Ophelia, with the help of a friend, Margot Joyes, for part of the time, had managed to bring up the children, look after my mother, run the home under conditions of scarcity, sell paintings and occasionally a print of 'Wind and Sun, Wastwater' (which we had published in case I did not return from the war), and to take her part in village life. She seemed to thrive on it all, but it was wonderful to be together again and to share the burdens, such as they were.

Margot, being about the same age as Ophelia, was a good friend, a tower of strength, and she loved and understood children. Once when we were all staying at Wood House, Buttermere, on our wedding anniversary, the 25th May, Margot said to Ophelia and me, 'You two go off for the day, and I will look after the children'. We didn't say where we were going, but, by mutual, consent, walked across the head of Crummock Water, passing the camp site of our honeymoon among the ancient hawthorns in full blossom with bluebells around their feet. To our utter amazement, we saw, written in pebbles on our camp site, the words 'May 25th, 1940'. It was like a miracle. Margot had gone the day before to the pebbly beach that joined Ling Crag to Melbreak, carried a load of pebbles in her skirt, nearly half a mile to the camp site and, having written, left the rest to chance and good planning.

Margot has continued to be a very good friend of our family right up to the present, and takes a lively interest in 'her children'.

Compared with that of most other families, our life was the most free of the usual material burdens, and those we had were mostly in the realm of the spirit and of our own making. One of the first hurdles of our life together was the discovery of the immense differences there were between our natures, and how

Buttermere Village (1969)

Shepherd and Lamb (1964)

we often misunderstood each other over quite simple things. When it came to an issue over which we both felt strongly it did not make it easier that we were both creative artists, and Ophelia was born under the sign of Leo and I under Libra.

I was the chief breadwinner, so it was often she who gave way, yet we both felt this wasn't good enough. After many years of trial and error, we began to find that the best shape for our life together was a triangle, with ourselves at each point of the baseline and God at the apex. Whenever we found that we were looking towards each other in irritation, anger or possessiveness – another form of the lust for power – we had to look up to the apex for an answer, and this gave us a clearer light on ourselves and each other. This we found mostly through regular times, early each morning, reading from the Bible, writing down any thoughts that came as being as near, in our present state, to being God's will, checking them with someone we trusted, and passing them on to others if needed. In this way we learned to live more by decision than by emotion alone. This interplay of emotion and decision, together with discipline, is the stuff of which a creative artist is made. If he didn't feel strongly about what he is making, no one else will feel much when they see it. Yet, without decision and discipline, it will lack conviction, form and design. It certainly needs a good deal of discipline for a sculptor, for instance, to work for years on a carving and, at the end, to convey in it what was her original inspiration, a well as what she has learned on the way.

Ophelia's uncle, Dr Saleeby, had died in the second year of the war, and her mother and aunt Muriel moved into a house at Heathwaite, above Windermere, adjoining the home of Aunt Dorothea. So there was a great deal of coming and going between Grasmere and Windermere, especially on such special occasions as Christmas, birthdays and the lovely and ancient ceremony of rushbearing in August. All the children of Grasmere make 'bearings' out of flowers (wild ones were the best), and rushes from the shores of the lakes of Grasmere and Rydal, made into the shapes of crosses and other emblems. They all process around the village to the music of the brass band, headed by the bishop and clergy and choir. They hold a short service in the church, the floor of which is covered with rushes, symbolic of the time when there was only an earth floor. As each child comes out, he or she is given a huge piece of fresh gingerbread and, on the following Monday, they hold a sports meeting, including a fell race for the children. The rushbearing ceremony is held each year on the Saturday nearest to August 5th, the day of Grasmere's patron saint, Saint Oswald.

One year, early in the 1940s, Ophelia modelled in plaster and painted figures for a Christmas crib – the baby Jesus, Mary, Joseph, and the shepherds, the kings and an ox and an ass – and a wooden barn was made by William Sharp, the village carpenter. This, and the Christmas tree, are the centrepieces of a service held each Christmas Eve, at which the children and the families of all ages are given a candle. After the brief service, the rector presses a button that switches

Tarn on Blake Rigg (1972)

on the lights in the crib and on a large Christmas tree near the altar. The Christmas of 1982 was the 40th anniversary of the Service of Blessing the Crib, and twelve of our family were there.

On Christmas Eve, 1940, Ophelia mentioned to the Rector that she had never been baptized, so this was done by candlelight that very same evening, Bernard and Dorothy Eyre Walker having been summoned from Langdale by telegram to act as Godparents. Later she was confirmed by Bishop Gresford-Jones at a lovely service in Grasmere church.

She was always delighted to tell people that she was married, baptized and confirmed, in that order, in our ancient village church.

SPRING, HEAD OF BUTTERMERE
(1982)

This was a still sunlit morning in mid-May, the loveliest time of the year, at the head of the most interesting of all the lake valleys in the district.

I woke up early, and knew exactly where I should go and paint. When I arrived at the head of the lake there were perfect mirror reflections on the water. I climbed from the road over a wire fence on to the sunlit fellside, new green grass just starting to rise between the washed-out reds of last year's bracken. The whole landscape was quiet and untenanted nature until I had my easel up, and started to draw in blue, violet and umber chalk pencils. Within minutes I was completely surrounded by sturdy Highland bullocks, just standing around out of curiosity.

I had no sooner shooed them well over the next rise and was flooding the first washes of sky and distance on to the paper when the first cars began to arrive. Soon the little car park was sparkling with metal, and then they started to park by the side of the road, between me and the reflections in the lake, that gradually changed as light breezes began to travel over the surface in fascinating blurred textures, leaving clear reflections close to the row of Scots pines that adds so much to the shingly shoreline.

The varied forms of the subject were, in themselves, complex and interesting, but the most attractive element was the light, that flooded the fellsides around Scarth Gap and added a warmth to the shadows of the Warnscale Crags. Each wash had to be kept on the light side to allow me to paint the stronger colours and tones of the foreground without having to make them too dark. Of course, the pure yellow of the gorse – cadmium mixed with aureolin – gave a clue to the brilliance of the clear morning sunlight, and the painting of it, in spite of a rather crowded foreground, was sheer delight. I was able to start and finish the painting on site, while the delight, controlled all the while by firm selection and organisation, was still with me.

Chapter 10
Home

Now that I was home again I was able to go out painting every possible day, so someone was needed to be in our gallery, to mount, frame and sell my paintings. We advertised for a studio manager.

The young man we chose out of twenty two applicants, John Bateman, had just left the army. He was a farmer's son from Hawkshead Hill so he knew the fells well, and he also had a deep feeling for good art. His energy was unbounded, and he could hardly bear to leave his work to catch the bus home, running out and leaping on to it as it passed the studio. He stayed with us for several years, until it became clear to us and to him that his considerable abilities could be used on a wider scale. He and his wife and four children emigrated to Canada. When they visited us a few years later, John had become a chairman of several companies in Canada.

I first met Ophelia's godfather, Bernard Eyre-Walker, at an Oxford Group weekend at Levens in 1934 at which, within two days, I made a decision about my life. Unlike me, Bernard went much more thoroughly and very honestly into the question of giving control of his whole life to God. For several years to come he was not quite sure about the existence of God, and he brought all kinds of troubles and tortures upon himself by this state of doubt. Certainty, however, came to him gradually over the years, and he became a tower of strength to his friends, greatly on account of his absolute integrity, which came out in his watercolours and etchings as well as in his life. He and I formed a deep, if difficult, friendship, difficult because our characters were so different. This showed, for instance, in the way we would set out to choose a subject for painting. On arriving at some interesting place I would joyfully sit down on my shooting stick and draw or paint the first thing that attracted me, while Bernard would spend at least half an hour prowling around like a lion stalking his prey until, having decided, he would paint a superb watercolour in half the time I would have taken. Every one of his brush strokes would have great content, as a result of his previous meditation, and seemed to convey the message. 'I know a lot more about it than this.' His work is in the great tradition of watercolour painters, from those of early China onwards. Several of his watercolours and etchings are in the Abbot Hall Art Gallery, Kendal, and I am the proud owner of a few.

Many of his most valuable thoughts came to him during the long watches of the night, especially during his long terminal illness. Several of them have been collected in a booklet named 'Quest', published in his memory by a painter friend, Rose Hugh-Jones.

He died in 1972 from cardiac asthma after a long and painful illness, during which he had to have a leg amputated to avoid gangrene.

Almost every year Ophelia and I took our growing family to Loweswater around the end of May, when the weather is usually fine, and because we liked it more that any other place in the world. At first we used to camp there, but, later, we came to know the Alexander family who live at Low Park, a rambling seventeenth century farm not far from the north western shore of Crummock Water. The Alexanders have an old shepherd's cottage in their farmyard and this they lent to their friends, so we spent many happy days in it, much of the time down by the ancient pele and its shingly bay. The hawthorn would be in blossom and the little valley of Rannerdale carpeted with bluebells.

A pele tower had been built on a promontory into the lake by Thomas de Lucy in the 13th century and a moat dug around it for protection in the times of raids from over the border. To this promontory would the neighbouring farmers drive their flocks and, to this day, it retains the feeling of sanctuary. In later years the pele tower was abandoned, and, out of it, on the same site, was built a farm. This, in turn, has fallen in ruins, so the grassy headland is now left to sheep and cattle. Beside a spring by the pebbly shore grows an ash tree as well as a few hawthorns. Among the boulders by the lake are some of pink granite and others of blue and green volcanic slate, brought down by glaciers from the fells around Buttermere, and the pebbles of softer Skiddaw slate have all been worn flat. They are perfect for endless games of ducks and drakes.

From this part of the valley the fells are seen to swoop down into the lake in graceful curves from Melbreak on the west to the Grasmoor group to the east. Standing well into the valley, usually against the light, is Rannerdale Knott, with its rocky side facing north. Away to the west stand Red Pike, High Stile, High

Bernard Eyre Walker (by Tom Dearden 1972)

Upstream in Rannerdale (1979)

Crag, the Haystacks, Brandreth and, beyond them all, Green and Great Gables seven miles away on the horizon. This makes a perfect natural composition, and I have painted it dozens of times at all times of the year and from dawn to after sunset, yet, for me, it is always new and entirely satisfying, and it fills my heart to be there.

Morning in Early Spring, Grasmere. (1969)

LANGDALE PIKES FROM LINGMOOR (1938)

This is the first of a series of eleven paintings I did of the same subject at different times of year and under different conditions, which was a useful bit of research as well as a most interesting and enjoyable exercise.

In abstract forms of art, a pyramid suggests strength and firmness – i.e. for mountains, broad based and part of the earth itself. A spiral suggests movement, and a right angle calm and repose.

In this subject all three of these shapes play their part, as illustrated in the margin – the curved run-in from the dark foreground, carried through into the sky, for it was a windy day full of movement. The pyramids, repeated from Side Pike in the middle distance on to Harrison Stickle, the highest point of the Langdale Pikes, flanked on each side by Pike of Stickle and Pavey Ark. To give the whole design an element of steadiness, there was a hint of the horizontal below the highest crags of the Pikes, and the dark cleft of Dungeon Ghyll supplied a useful vertical.

Although this was started and finished on site, I had begun it with these basic shapes in mind and so was able to stress them in the whole painting. Afterwards, at home, I made a few sketches of different stages in the painting, two of which are shown in the margin.

It has always been my aim to design a painting when working from nature, and also to capture some spontaneity when working in the studio from a sketch or from memory or imagination. Without a good design, the result is never any good.

The day of the painting was in November, a day of much movement. I started with sky and distances in cool grey washes, gradually introducing warmer local colours toward the middle distance and, finally, painting in the rich dark heather in the foreground in great washes of burnt sienna and alizarin crimson mixed with ultramarine, the rocks a cooler mixture of burnt sienna and ultramarine.

This was the first time I had gone out painting with the woman who was to become my wife, and this gave me courage and joy.

I gave the painting to the Fell and Rock Club, and it now hangs in our hut at Wasdale Head.

Chapter 11

Mountain Painting

Design for Plate 66

First Stage

Near same subject in November (1940)

I am often asked how I set about choosing a subject in a part of the country that has such a rich variety in its permanent forms, as well as a continuously changing light passing over and among them.

Over the years of living in this Lake District I have kept my eyes open as I go about among the fells, and made mental notes of the places from which the forms come together to make an interesting design in three dimensions, for without good design the first ingredient of a work of art is missing.

I like to wake early, look at the weather conditions, decide what it might do during the day, after some meditation decide on a likely subject and, when I have got my painting kit together, set off on foot, or in my car, to the nearest point it will take me to choose my subject. If it involves walking or climbing for some distance, I keep on the look-out for any subject that is especially interesting under the prevailing conditions, and I reserve for myself the freedom to abandon or postpone my originally intended subject if need be. In fact, to be a complete opportunist.

Of course this means, for me, the experience of over sixty years of painting in this small group of hills, training the visual memory to decide on the choice of subject, while taking into account the position of the sun and the character of the sky. Living, as I do, almost in the middle of the Lake District, I can reach by car even the farthest valley heads in about an hour and a half. This includes Wasdale Head if I drive over Wrynose and Hardknott Passes, and the head of Ennerdale, for which I have been given by the Forestry Commission special permission to take a car.

In fact for me the Lake District is just the right size and shape to be accessible from my home.

Of course, when I want to paint from dawn onwards, I either stay in a local house near my subject or, better still, camp with a tent or motor caravan, from the inside of which I can paint in rainy weather, and there is something intangible to be gained by spending the night close to the subject.

It seems to me now that, after having been attracted to the climbing of mountains for its own sake, I climbed increasingly in order to find interesting angles on the surrounding terrain. In the end, landscape painting in mountain country depends upon training the visual memory through constant practice.

In the late l940s I decided to make an experiment of painting more-or-less the same subject at different times of year under different conditions of weather and time of day. I needed a subject in which the permanent solid forms made an interesting design in three dimensions, so I chose the view of the Langdale Pikes from the ridge of Lingmoor. From there one sees the Pikes at right angles to their general slope, so that the true rhythms and proportions of the subject are best revealed, rather than from the valley below, from which the foothills can easily appear out of proportion to the whole.

In the middle distance stood Side Pike, with its vertical rock faces contrasting with the rounded sides towards the valley, where the glaciers have smoothed off the rocks or left their debris. There is, in this subject, an interesting balance between straight lines and curves, seen as an abstract design yet, with the straight lines revealing the 'parent' rock, part of the earth's bony structure, and the curves representing the muscles, the debris left behind by glacial action. I have found this distinction between bones and muscles very helpful when confronted by a mountain mass which, at first sight, seems rather chaotic and complex.

Altogether I made eleven studies in this series of paintings, and the exercise taught me, among other things, how different the same subject can appear under different conditions.

Claude Monet made a similar experiment with his series of 'Rheims Cathedral,' 'Haystacks' and 'Poplars', and, best of all, the late series of paintings of the lily pond in his garden. And, of course, Cézanne painted his beloved Mont Sainte Victoire very many times under different conditions.

The technique of watercolour is not an easy one to master, yet, for me, it is eminently right for the landscape of England, and especially of the Lake District, which is often reduced, in the distances, to subtle almost – yet not quite – flat washes. This is due to the moisture contained in the air, drawn by the sun from the quantities of standing or running water among the hills.

Usually, when I am painting out-of-doors, I start by drawing the design of the work in pencil or blue and brown chalk, mainly to establish the main forms on the rectangle. I find the best paper for my purposes is Green's Bockingford for swift direct sketches, and R.W.S. 'Not' surface, 140lb or 300lbs, made also by J. Barcham Green and Sons of Maidstone. The thicker paper acts as a kind of reservoir for great washes, allowing one time to add drier colour to them while the paper is still really wet.

The size I like best is round about 22 inches by 15, which is just about as much as I see in one eyeful at arms' stretch without moving my head, but on occasions I work twice that size or larger, or even half that size. I do not often paint any smaller, except on the occasion of having been invited by the president of the Royal Institute to contribute a watercolour for an album, to which other members contributed, as a wedding present for the Prince and Princess of Wales in July 1981. The size of this was 7 inches by 5½. I remembered that Prince Charles had driven in a yellow open touring Rolls Royce over Kirkstone Pass to open a Maritime Museum on the shore of Windermere. From just below the top of Red Screes I painted the dark crag of Kilnshaw Chimney against the distant Windermere winding towards a golden sky with showers in columns against the light. Down below, the road of Kirkstone Pass appeared, so I hope it may have brought back some memory to Prince Charles. I received a very nice letter from our president, Charles Bone, saying how much the royal couple liked it and would continue to enjoy it. Prince Charles had sent some of his own watercolours to the Institute's 1980 exhibition, and also to the exhibition of 1982, and has now become an honorary member.

I use only Russian Sable brushes, starting usually with large brushes, either filbert of flat one-stroke, laying in the sky and distances and all pale large surfaces first, playing about while wet by brushing or dropping darker drier

Sketch for Windermere from Red Screes (1981)

colour into the washes. As my washes become darker in a foreground, I work with smaller brushes and drier colour, much in the way the traditional Chinese worked. If my big brush has a good point, I find I can paint almost the whole picture with the one brush.

However, there are occasions when one needs to abandon this traditional technique. For instance, one evening in May I had been painting with my friend, Ronald Mann, all day on Torver Moor above Coniston Water and, as we were packing up, I thought it might be worth while to go round to the eastern shore of the lake and look at a subject I had in mind. We arrived at the spot just as the evening sun was raking with a low cross light over what I think is one of the finest skylines in England, that of the Coniston fells, from Brown Pike and Dow Crag, over the curved pyramid of the Old Man to Brim Fell, Swirl How and Wetherlam. The foreground was a couple of rocky headlands and the middle distance the lower silurian-stone moorlands leading up to the higher fells.

I knew the light would only last about half an hour, so I drew everything in blue, violet and umber conté pencils, then painted in only the shadows of the whole subject.

At home in my studio a few days later – to give time for the paint to harden – I laid in the whole picture with a golden evening light, working very swiftly so as not to disturb the shadow washes beneath, and varied this, in differing ways, right up to the sharp foreground rocks and golden-green grass, never touching the paper with a second wash.

Again, I suggest that each subject must be allowed to dictate design and treatment, so that every painting becomes a new and exciting adventure.

I think the sort of mountain country in which I like best to paint is from some high broad ridge containing one or more tarns, and looking across to higher mountains, such as one sees the craggy north side of Fairfield from Angle Tarn above Patterdale, or the Langdale Pikes group, Bowfell and the Coniston Fells from the ridge of Blake Rigg, with its several rock-bound tarns that, like eyes of

The Island, Grasmere (1973)

Dawn Light on Mont Blanc (1956)

the mountain, bring some of the sky right down to the foreground. And, of course, there are countless places in the Lake District where a lake forms a splendid foreground to mountains.

I have never achieved anything approaching a high degree of proficiency in rock climbing or mountaineering. The highest standard of rock climbing I have ever led is the standard of 'very severe', though I have followed leaders on 'exceptionally severe' routes. But I have always enjoyed climbing rocks and mountains from the time when, in my teens, I went alone because I did not know anyone who cared for climbing, and my parents strongly opposed rock climbing on a rope.

Apart from the expeditions with highly experienced climbers while illustrating the rock climbing guides to the Lake District, my mountain climbing in England and Scotland, Norway, the Alps and the Andes has been mostly with the aim of painting from them. I find that one gets the best view of a mountain from another opposite, and equal to about half the height of the former, being, as it were, at right angles to its general slope. This is not to say that great views of mountains cannot be obtained from the summits or from the lower levels, even from flat valleys or lakes. For instance, I have found great satisfaction in painting the Mont Blanc massif and the Chamonix and Argentières pinnacles from the ridge of the Aiguilles Rouges, across the Chamonix Valley; the Matterhorn from Findelen or the Gornergrat, from whence I have also painted that queen among mountains, the Weisshorn; the Dom ridge from above Saas Almagen or from the Portiengrat; and, in Norway, the Smörstabbtinder and Fanaraaken from Sognefjell; the Skagastölstinder from above Turtagrö; Trolltindener from Trolstigheimen; and, in our own Lake District, the Langdale Pikes from Lingmoor or from Blake Rigg; the Scafell group from Hardknott Fell or from Great Gable, and vice versa; Bowfell from Gimmer Crag or thereabouts; Helvellyn from Place Fell or Caudale Moor; Blencathra from the Dodds or Naddle Fell, and so on. Of course the Cuillin Ridge of Skye is best seen from the ridge itself, though good views of it can be seen from Ben Staic

Matterhorn from Gornergrat (1956)

and An Cruachan, Elgol and Ord. In Wales, the surrounding mountains, especially Y Garn, look very fine from the top of Tryfan or from the Carnedds.

So far I have not written anything about trying to interpret the fleeting effects of changing light on the permanent forms of the mountains. For this I have had the experience of sixty-five years in which to train my visual memory. I watch until the effect of light most fully brings out the character of the subject, and, thereafter, translate whatever happens into the memory of what I decided, trying never to change my mind halfway through but using the landscape as reference for my translation. Some people, of course, don't take so long to train their visual memory, but it is really on visual memory that painting out-of-doors in mountain country depends.

I find that I can remember colour and tone more readily than form, especially the intricate sculpture of the Lakeland fells, so, if the conditions don't allow me to paint in full colour, I find, if I can get a thoroughly understood drawing, perhaps in blue and sepia and black chalk pencils, I have won half the battle, and can do a painting in full colour in my studio. And occasionally I paint entirely from memory or from imagination, which is very exciting.

Painters of Lakeland for many years have produced sometimes fantastic caricatures of our fells in order to impress. Personally I have too much respect for each one of them. They are my old friends whom I can recognise from all kinds of odd viewpoints. For me, because I know them so well, it seems important to preserve for them 'a local habitation and a name'.

GRASMERE FROM HELM CRAG
(1963)

It was a clear, still frosty morning in February when I woke with the thought of painting the Lion and the Lamb and all the tumbled rocks of the strange rift through the summit of the mountain, the sort of thing an axe does to a log.

By the time I had climbed up from Easdale, there was already a hint of warmth in the unbroken sunlight. The sounds from the valley reached me very faintly, and were soon forgotten, when I set up my easel and started painting. The west wind had carved the snow into sharp sculptured edges that stood out dramatically in contrast with the gentle rolling distances to the south.

First I drew the whole subject in Derwent Crayons, blue and violet in the distances and umber and black in the foreground. Then I washed in the sky, very wet, gradating from palest cobalt blue down to the horizon in light red and vermilion with a touch of cobalt, quickly running over the sunlit lowlands with palest light red, including the island. When this was dry I put in Grasmere Lake with cobalt and a hint of aureolin yellow. Then came the pale shadows of the distances, swift washes of cobalt and alizarin crimson.

To accentuate the contrast of the shadowed Lion I put its shadow in, full strength in one wash of cobalt and light red, slightly colder and greyer than the distant shadows, and swiftly painted the Lamb and the rocks and ridges of the foreground, finally dashing in the half-tones in the same colour.

Finally came the rocks, those in sunlight a slightly warm mixture of burnt sienna with a touch of ultramarine, in shadow the same mixture but colder and darker.

The whole painting was completed in not much more than an hour, so it has the vigour and conviction of a watercolour started and finished in front of the subject. The white of the snow in sun is untouched paper.

A spontaneous statement such as this gives a chance for the paper to play its part as it reflects light through the various washes.

Chapter 12

Winterseeds

On June 10th 1947 we were blessed with another son, Julian Gordon, and, on August 17th 1949, another daughter, Clare Ophelia Gordon. By this time it was obvious that the little house attached to the studio was rather cramped for a family of seven, for my mother was still living with us.

About a mile north of Grasmere village, above the main road to Keswick, stood a house named Winterseeds that had been rented for fifty years by John Haden Badley, the founder of Bedales School, the first co-educational boarding school in Britain. During school holidays he and his wife would often bring some of the pupils to their Grasmere home, and Badley's two sisters, Laura and Mary, lived at Winterseeds all the year round.

The name of the house was derived from the old Norse words 'vind erg saetr', meaning a high windy dairy farm, built probably betwen 800 and 1000 AD. In the seventeenth century a farm was built in stone upon the foundations of the wooden Norse building.

For many years Winterseeds belonged to the Wilsons, an old Grasmere yeoman family. Towards the end of the nineteenth century, the Wilsons built on to the dwelling house portion, almost doubling its size and turning it into a fine private house. Since the Badleys had occupied it, they had built onto it a wing to the south – a library and two more bedrooms – so the house had three reception rooms, eight bedrooms, three lavatories and one tiny bathroom almost filled by an enormous bath made of sheet copper, which was supposed to be good in relieving rheumatism.

When the Badley sisters were in their nineties Miss Laura died and Miss Mary decided to end her days in a nursing home, so Mrs Ann Wilson, the owner, decided to let Winterseeds.

Ophelia and I walked up the steep 150 yard drive to see it, and we both liked it very much, but I thought there would be a waiting list and, also, that Ophelia would never be able to push a pram up the steep drive. She, however, had immediately fallen in love with the house and everything about it. There was a quarter of an acre of well-stocked though rather wild garden, on slopes and terraces with rocks and trees among them. The Badley sisters had been keen

Wetherlam from Langdale Fell (1973)

gardeners. Besides the house with its great farm kitchen and three cool larders, there were several stone outhouses and, across the yard, a great barn of dry stone walling that had fallen into ruin.

Ophelia told me later that she started to pray that we should live there, feeling confident that this would happen. I learned that there was a waiting list of six would-be tenants, so I thought that we were too late, but I added my name to it.

One evening a message arrived from old Mrs Wilson, the owner, asking if I would go up and see her in Easdale. To my astonishment she told me that we could rent Winterseeds for ten years for the annual rent of £150! Years later we learned that the reason she had chosen us sprang from a wish of Miss Badley's that ours should be the family who should live there.

So we decided to move in at once, as the new baby, Clare, was only three months old. We arranged for my mother, who was now bedridden with arthritis, to live with a nurse in Grasmere, by whom she could be looked after professionally. At the sale of the Badley's large furniture we were able to buy a lot of it, thanks to many Grasmere residents who kept the bidding low.

Strange to say, for several years, while Miss Mary Badley was still living in a nursing home in Ambleside, we used to hear her going from her bedroom to the bathroom. We became so used to this sound that we took it for granted as quite normal, but, on one occasion, when our son-in-law, Peter Johnson, was baby-sitting, he heard her and became alarmed, and crept upstairs holding a poker. He was even more alarmed to find no one there. After her death she ceased to visit her old home. This was our nearest encounter with a ghost, and such a pleasant one.

We turned the largest front bedroom into a studio for me to paint in. In order to diffuse the sunlight through the large bay windows that faced south-west, I hung muslin curtains over them. This produced a slightly warm light that approximated to a lively normal daylight, which I prefer to the rather dead north light used by portrait painters. We turned one bedroom into a second bathroom and the children each had their own bedrooms. The large library made a wonderful play room for them, and they could come and go into the garden through the window.

Over the years we were fortunate in employing young girls, mostly Swiss, to help Ophelia with the house and the children. This continued in our new home and we were able to invite many friends to stay with us, some from wearying life in busy industrial centres, and some very delightful painters, including Adrian Allinson, and Dr Kenneth McAll, the leading psychiatrist who had learned to paint in China.

Adrian was in his sixties when we first met him through a sculpture of his in the Royal Academy. He exhibited often in the R.A., and was a member of the Society of Painters, Etchers and Engravers.

He lived, painted and entertained in his commodious studio in St Johns Wood. I recall the first meal that Ophelia and I had with him there – an enjoyable and inventive dinner, entirely vegetarian, which he had cooked himself. After dinner he told us of his belief in incarnation, and, quite seriously, he told me that I was the incarnation of a Buddhist monk of the first century.

Adrian loved painting the early spring. He would start painting in the southern counties, moving on with the spring to us in Grasmere, on to a friend's house at Alston, a high moorland town in north-east Cumberland, and then on, with the spring, into Scotland.

His paintings, always oils, had a strong feeling for design, while he had learned very much from the Post-Impressionists, Van Gogh and Gauguin.

On his last stay with us he announced that he was coming to live with us, and Ophelia found it very hard to tell him that she had already four children, so we could not have him.

Kenneth McAll was already an experienced doctor and psychiatrist when I first met him. He and his wife, Frances, had been running a hospital in China at the time of the Japanese invasion. At one time, when the hospital was on the battle line, they used to go out after a battle and pick up the wounded. On one of these occasions they found a Chinese soldier and nursed him for two years back to health. This man, who never told them his name, was a highly accomplished painter, and he taught Ken to paint in the traditional method of the Chinese schools.

Winterseeds Welcome (1950)

Ophelia, Heaton, Julian and Clare (1954)

Weisshorn from Gornergrat (1955)

Eventually, the McAlls and their six-month-old daughter, Elizabeth, were interned in a factory in Shanghai, together with 1200 others of 38 nationalities. They were there for 4½ years, and Ken used his gift as a painter to communicate to their fellow prisoners first the rules of hygiene, and eventually the instructions of the elected prisoners' parliament, so ensuring their physical, moral and spiritual welfare over the years. His picture messages were painted on packing paper by means of soot, lime and charcoal.

During this time he kept a picture diary, painted on the leaves of a toilet roll, and this was included in an exhibition at the Alpine Club Gallery in London.

We were always glad when Ken came to stay, and he was a great inspiration to Ophelia right up to the end of her life.

The McAlls and their five children went to live in Conan Doyle's former home near Lyndhurst in the New Forest. Frances has a busy practice as a general practitioner, still having time and energy to write books on physical and spiritual well-being, while Ken has become known world-wide as a psychiatrist and also for his ability to exorcise evil spirits, in conjunction with the church.

While in the USA, having been invited by N.A.S.A., as a painter and psychiatrist, to choose the colours for the interior of the Skylab before the first moon landing, while being shown designs for the Moonrover and watching its performance, he had an inner conviction that its nitrogen-filled Goodyear tyres could be a danger were they to be punctured. He drew a sketch of 'wheels with coiled springs connecting the axle to a perforated metal strip which would act as a tyre'. His design was adopted. This and other more important experiences are described in his recent book – 'Healing the Family Tree'. (*Sheldon Press SPCK, 1982*).

Owing to Ophelia's parents having separated when she was three years old, she used to suffer sometimes from almost hopeless depression, and, at those times, she felt quite sure that she was a complete failure as a wife, mother and artist. I remember one night, some years after our marriage, after one of her times of utter depression, when we were asleep, I woke up suddenly to see a form, black and like an octopus, hovering over our bed. I was so terrified that I could only repeat 'Jesus, Jesus', and it suddenly disappeared. Ever since that happening I have never doubted the existence of evil spirits or an evil spirit.

During my work in Air Ministry I came to know Wing Commander Athol Murray. When the post of studio manager fell vacant he offered himself for it, so

Steel Fell Tarn (1962)

he and his wife, Olive, lived in our former home at the studio, and he ran the business. He was a superb photographer, so he knew what made a good painting, and he was able to mount and frame watercolours. He loved walking on the fells, and he liked people, so the business was in good hands and I was freed to paint and write.

My first book achieved a second edition in 1947 and we expanded into publishing more colour prints from my Lakeland paintings, reaching a large public who could not afford originals. Our colour printers, W S Cowell Ltd, of Ipswich, were considered to be the finest in Britain.

In 1954 I wrote a second book, 'Lakeland Portraits', that dealt more personally and in more detail with five chosen areas of the district. In 1960 I wrote a third book, 'The Tarns of Lakeland', which described all 144 named tarns that constitute some of the most delightful features of the district. At the end of each chapter, I gave details of maximum depth, height above sea level, surface area and map reference, and this has been for many years the standard work on the subject. This book also ran to two editions and many people found in it an object for their fell walks, often seeing how many tarns they could visit on each of their holidays. I wrote a fourth book, 'The Lakes', in 1966 with information about the fourteen lakes that had not appeared in print before, and a good deal of first-hand experience from over sixty-five years of walking and painting. This also ran into two editions. The writing of these books brought to me another dimension of my understanding of the district, especially along the lines of geology, archaeology and history. They were all fully illustrated with drawings and paintings, which were for me the most enjoyable part of the operation.

On April 27th, 1953, my mother passed away peacefully at the age of ninety. She was buried with her husband in the churchyard of St. Mary's, Ambleside.

In 1938 a Major John Hunt and his wife, Joy, had stayed for a month in Grasmere, and I came to know them through walking on the fells, with an occasional rock climb. Even as early as 1938 he was thinking of Everest, and he asked if I would come as artist to a possible future expedition. I said I was too old, and anyway had not the physical stamina. But this was typical of his character, to expect the utmost and the best from his friends, and so often he got it.

In May 1953 Colonel John Hunt led the expedition that climbed Everest for the first time, and in August of the same year Sir John Hunt invited Ophelia and myself and the Osmastons for the day to the Outward Bound Mountain School in Eskdale, where his old friend, Eric Shipton, was warden, and where the whole of the Everest team, except Tensing, was holding a reunion. The weather behaved abominably as it does sometimes in August and some of the party had

Blaven, Skye. (1982)

The Osmastons. (1983)

spent the morning in canoes, shooting the rapids of the swollen River Esk. Edmund Hillary overturned and was nearly drowned. George Lowe lost his false teeth which were discovered washed up on some shingle lower down the river!

Ophelia was very impressed with Hillary, and soon afterwards modelled in clay a very vigorous portrait of him, which she then cast in plaster. This was almost the first sculpture she had done since we were married thirteen years ago. She herself agreed with everyone that it was the best portrait she had ever done, and she said that, instead of having lost any of her skill, her work had improved and had a richer content, due to her experience as a wife and mother. The bronze of this portrait now resides in the National Gallery of New Zealand at Wellington.

The next portrait she did was of John Hunt, and for this we stayed with him and his wife, Joy, and their four daughters at Camberley, where John was Assistant Commandant of the Staff College. In 1955 John drove from Camberley to open an exhibition, at the Fine Art Society in Bond Street, of paintings of mine and a few sculptures by Ophelia, including the portrait of Hillary. This, my third one–man exhibition in London, had a quite reasonable success.

One summer, when John and Joy and their daughter, Susan, were on an expedition in Greenland, we had their two younger daughters, Prue and Jenny, to stay with us for three weeks at Winterseeds, then we went en famille to their home, Highway Cottage, Aston, on the Thames, two miles below Henley. Another year, John, Joy and Susan camped for two weeks in the field beside Winterseeds. The weather was glorious and we had many enjoyable days on the fells, swimming in the tarns between climbs.

Our two sons, John and Julian, began their education at the primary school in Grasmere, while our two daughters, Otalia and Clare, started at the primary school, Fairfield, attached to the Parents National Education Union, (P.N.E.U.)

Young Wordsworth (1972)

Training College at Scale How, Ambleside. This college is now the Charlotte Mason College of Education, named after the founder of the P.N.E.U. system. The boys went on to Earnseat Preparatory School at Arnside on the Kent Estuary. Otalia stayed on at the P.N.E.U. College until she was seventeen, and Clare went as a boarder to Kendal High School. The boys went on to Heversham, a boarding grammar school some 25 miles from Grasmere, near enough for us to take part in school affairs and to get to know the staff.

We stayed our ten years at Winterseeds, and another three years until our children were fairly well launched, and then, in 1962, we moved back to our studio house again.

The Winterseeds years were some of our happiest. It was a very friendly house, above the valley mist and below the mountain mist, with plenty of space and fells and sky around it, receiving a lot of sun. For two weeks in June we enjoyed three sunsets every day as the sun disappeared behind various bits of Helm Crag across the valley.

We took the children during the holidays on several camping trips to the sea at Drigg, on the West Cumberland coast, when few people knew about the splendid sands and the bird sanctuary there. In a snowy winter we would ski and toboggan and, all the other months, go together on the fells and into the tarns. These were some of the happiest days of our lives together.

Kentmere from High Street. (1957)

PILLAR MOUNTAIN FROM FLEETWITH (1953)

Cloud banks still covered the tops when I started to climb Fleetwith, but, by the time I reached its summit, the west wind from the sea had begun to roll them away like blankets.

Pillar Mountain dominated the view to the north, its long rising ridge, with deep combes gouged out by glaciers from its sides, came to a climax in its blunt summit, with Pillar Rock standing upright between two dark combes, its top just catching the sun.

The whole subject was very majestic, from the foreground of rocks, grass and heather in sunlight, on to the blue-black ridge of Haystacks, its sunlit tops of heather in light and Warnscale Crags very dark. Then, beyond all this, Pillar Mountain.

I started by drawing in the main shapes with blue, grey and black chalks. Then came the sky, painted all in one wash by adding darker and bluer colours to the right. Next came the shadowed bulk of Pillar Mountain, painted from left to right, becoming slightly paler with distance, all in variations of cobalt and light red.

Next came the Haystacks ridge, for which I used ultramarine and light red, adding some burnt sienna on the nearer crags. This needed to be dark enough to send Pillar a mile or two farther behind it, yet still atmospheric when compared with the warm blacks of the foreground shadows, painted in burnt sienna and ultramarine and occasionally Winsor blue.

Having established the shadows, which made the subject so dramatic, I began to paint the sunlit edges, first with pale burnt sienna on Pillar, then with slightly warm purply grey for the heathery summits of Haystacks, and, finally, with pale raw and burnt sienna and aureolin in the foreground.

I gave this final version to the Royal Institute as my diploma painting. Also, I painted a large oil, commissioned by the firm of Guest, Keen and Nettlefold, in memory of one of their laboratory staff who was killed while climbing in the Himalayas.

Chapter 13

Commissions

One evening when I was staying alone at the Strands Hotel, Nether Wasdale, painting Wastwater and the fells around, two men arrived for the night and, after dinner, we talked about this and that and I don't remember what.

Three years later one of the men, T. L. Viney, 'phoned to ask me if I would be willing to paint a very large watercolour of a nuclear station to be built at Dounreay, close to Thurso on the north east coast of Scotland. The installation did not yet exist, but I should be expected to paint it from plans and models. The purpose of the painting was to show it to a conference of world scientists assembled at Geneva in 1954, to plan the next steps in harnessing nuclear power for peaceful purposes. The Chairman of the Atomic Energy Authority, Sir Christopher Hinton, accepted that position on condition that at least half the work of the A.E.A. was to be devoted to peaceful purposes, and it was he who wanted the painting.

I agreed to take on the commission and flew up to Dounreay to make studies of the coastline on which the installation was to be built. It was a period of stormy weather in March, with black hail storms coming out of the north, and, between them, great shafts of sunlight flashing on to the rocky coast. These gleams of light gave me the inspiration for the message of the painting, which was that light is stronger than darkness, and that the light of heaven could include the works of man as well as those of the Creator.

There was at that time great difficulty in obtaining large sheets of good watercolour paper of the size I needed, 40 inches by 30, but I had managed to obtain one sheet. A great deal of the painting consisted of sky of a very complex character, for it was to show a great wide ray of light, slightly to the left of centre, and, on the right, great black hail showers coming charging out of the Orkneys in the north, indicating the sort of troublous times we live in and should expect in the future.

As the sky had to be painted very swiftly while the paint was still wet, in not much more than five minutes, I prayed for courage, and I asked Ophelia and a Swiss girl, who were working downstairs in the kitchen, to pray like anything. The sky seemed to paint itself.

At the time of the Geneva conference on Nuclear Power for Peaceful Purposes I was staying at Mountain House, the European headquarters of Moral Re-armament, at Caux, above the lake of Geneva. I took with me a friend, Peter Phelps, to lunch in the Palais des Nations. We met there many scientists from all over the world and I was asked to speak to them on the significance of the painting. Many years later, in the Atticus column of the 'Sunday Times', in an interview Lord Hinton told the story of the painting that now hung in his office of the Central Electricity Generating Board, of which he was Chairman, He told Atticus that 'the man who painted it was very religious; but it's a very good painting'. Over the next few years I was commissioned by the

Pillar Mountain from Fleetwith (Oil) (1955)

Sketch for Dounreay Nuclear Power Station (1954)

Dolphins and Merchild (1963)

AEA to paint large watercolours of Windscale, Calder Hall, Chapel Cross and Harwell, and eventually an oil painting of the occasion when the Queen switched on the first electric power from atomic energy at Calder Hall.

In the meantime the A.E.A. had become interested in Ophelia's sculpture. First they commissioned a series of three panels in low relief, carved in stone, showing the various stages in the production of nuclear power. These panels are now in the entrance hall of the headquarters of the A.E.A. Industrial Group at Risley in Lancashire.

Next they commissioned a bronze fountain of dolphins for a research station at Winfrith Heath in Dorset, and, in 1960, they asked her to carve two large stone figures, to be placed on each side of the entrance to their headquarters at Risley. We thought this out together, seeking guidance on the whole question of the use and misuse of power. One of the figures kneeling was that of Man holding a symbol of the unbroken atom and seeking guidance from God on how it was to be used. The other figure, half kneeling, was Man in action, placing a symbolic control rod into a symbolic nuclear reactor. This involved a journey to the Isle of Portland to choose two suitable blocks of white stone, each weighing about four tons. When the ten-ton low-loading lorry arrived with the stone it refused to go up our steep drive. Ophelia showed the men how they could winch their lorry up by running a cable round a tree, which they did with success, though rather sheepishly!

Saint Bede (1964)

For this commission she had re-built the old stone barn adjoining the house, incorporating large roof lights and thick beams to which she attached pulleys. The two blocks of stone were placed on iron wheeled trolleys. In order to speed up the initial roughing-out stages she used an electrically powered chisel, but, when that was done, she took to the wooden mallet and various cold steel chisels. All the while the wind blew through one dry stone wall and out of the other. The work took her eighteen months to complete, working for several hours almost every day. Along a beam in her studio she wrote a line from a favourite hymn, 'Unresting, unhasting, as silent as light'.

Her next carving commission was for a Saint Bede, to be placed on a tower of a new Roman Catholic church in Carlisle. This was carved in hard white Roman stone. The completed sculpture was lifted by a crane on to its pedestal on the face of the tower. Ophelia climbed up to it by a ladder and, while she was removing its wrappings, I went out into Wigton Road to see how it looked to passers by. Two men were also watching, and one of them turned to me saying. 'Do you see yon young woman up there? She did it.' my reply was: 'Yes, I know, she's my wife, and we three are the first people in the world to see that sculpture in its place.' They looked at my greying hairs and moved quickly away. During this time she carried out several portraits, one of them a commission for a portrait of Wordsworth in his twenties, when he was living in Grasmere and writing his best verse. No portrait of him at this period of his life existed, so she had to work from her imagination, referring to the bony structure of his portraits painted in later life.

Poem (1965)

For several years she modelled studies of shepherds – some with dogs, sheep or lambs – climbers, young couples, and one of William and Dorothy Wordsworth walking in the wind. One particularly interesting group was inspired by a young man and a girl sitting in front of us in church, listening to Richard Wordsworth reciting poems by his great-great-grandfather, William. We never saw their faces, but she managed to convey the feeling of two young people aware of each other and, at the same time, aware of the poetry. She called the sculpture 'Poem'.

These sculptures were first modelled in clay on an aluminium armature, then cast in plaster and finally cast in cold-cast bronze. Each subject was limited to an edition of twelve to comply with the definition of an original work, laid down by the Royal Society of British Sculptors. One of the commissions she enjoyed very much was for a Madonna and Child for the chapel of the convent of Saint Denys in Warminster.

In the late 1960s she welded together some scrap metal she picked up from the floor of the village smithy. Out of this she created a figure of Christ on the cross, the figure being a space in the centre, of human shape with arms outstretched, the surrounding cross being made of sharp cruel shapes of metal, including a number of radiating nails. This was shown in the summer exhibition of the Lake Artists Society in Grasmere Hall. One woman who saw it commissioned a larger version, some seven feet in height, to be placed on the roof of the chapel of the Dorothy Kerrin Home of Healing at Burrswood, Groombridge, Kent.

Breakthrough (1967)

Ophelia built up this version from pieces of aluminium that she found in car breakers' yards. While she was making it, our village doctor, Ben Alexander and his wife, Margaret, who were also our next door neighbours, were facing a decision about an invitation given them by the Salvation Army to run one of their hospitals in Pakistan, though neither of them had lived elsewhere than in England.

Watching Ophelia building up the figure of Christ from cruel broken pieces of scrap metal seemed to clear the issue for them. At their farewell party in the village hall, Ben spoke of how her sculpture had been the inspiration behind their acceptance of the hospital post. He called the sculpture 'Breakthrough' and so it has come to be known in its home in Kent. Apparently it arrived at the time Burrswood was going through a period of crisis after the death of its founder, Dorothy Kerrin, so it was a breakthrough for the staff, and, since then, has continued to help many to health as they see it from the terrace with the Kentish sky shining through the figure.

For some years I had been holding painting courses for a week each in spring and autumn, using a greenhouse as a studio when rain stopped work outside. Usually some twenty or so students of all ages came to them, and, in the evenings,

I would give illustrated talks on various aspects of art. I enjoyed them as well as the students, especially as, on each afternoon, I did a demonstration of painting out of doors.

There was, and needed to be, as little organisation as possible about these painting courses. After meeting at ten o'clock we would all go to some place, not too far away, at which were numerous choices of subject, for I felt it was important for each pupil to make all decisions possible, especially choosing a subject and designing the painting. I would resist answering questions like, 'How do I paint this rock?' but try to encourage pupils to express their own feelings instead of producing second-hand Heaton Coopers. Really, I would answer their questions by my demonstration after they had done their own painting in their own way. On the last morning of the course we held an exhibition of all the week's work by every pupil, and I would criticise, encourage and suggest directions for further study. Besides forming a fruitful, (for I learned a lot), and enjoyable week together, good lasting friendships were cemented that have stood the test of time as people came year after year and met each other again. In 1964 we decided to add to the building a working studio for me and the students to paint in, the whole of the roof being of perspex to give an even top light.

Over the years I held one-man exhibitions in London, Manchester, Leeds, Newcastle, Chester and two in Liverpool, all of which were quite successful and helped to inform people of my work, but the most effective place for sales of paintings, prints and books has always been our gallery in Grasmere.

Since Ophelia and I published our first colour print, "Wind and Sun, Wastwater", in 1940, the print publishing business at the Studio has steadily grown until, at the moment, it includes 80 titles, by far the greatest collection of colour prints of the Lake District from contemporary paintings.

The print business has freed me more and more to paint "from the heart" without having to paint "potboilers" or to repeat a painting in order to be sure of the money. Out of the thousands of paintings I have produced over 65 years, when choosing which painting to reproduce, we have chosen subjects, usually of lakes, which we think might sell in thousands in order to recoup the considerable outlay of publishing prints of the highest quality, each carefully checked by us in the proofing stage. At present the staff of the Studio is comprised of six full time and three part time members, Richard Hardisty and my eldest son John, being joint managers.

So, because of the commercial publishing of prints, I am freed to experiment and to paint ever new subjects, each painting being for me a new discovery, adventure and challenge.

Scafell Pike and Lingcove Beck (1967)

THE CUILLIN RIDGE FROM LOCH HARPORT, SKYE (1982)

In October of 1982 I was staying with two climbing friends at Carbost, the village that, for fifty years, I have found to be the most strategically placed for reaching, with the help of a car, either end of the Cuillin ridge. Each day a ceiling of cloud hung over the whole or part of the bristling crest of the Cuillin. My friends, Bill and Enid Comstive, climbed in spite of cloud, while I explored the neighbourhood for an interesting foreground and middle distance that could lead up to a view of the whole ridge. This I found at Ullinish, on the northern shore of Loch Harport at the corner where it turns south into Bracadale Bay.

I went there several times, making drawings of the stretch of loch leading up to the Cuillin, of the rounded basalt moorlands in the middle distance, but the Cuillin refused to appear. Then, one morning, the easterly wind lifted the cloud base at the western end of the ridge, revealing Sgurr Alasdair as the true and most pointed summit. Whenever the whole ridge is clear, the high points at each end are Sgurr Alasdair and Sgurr nan Gillean, leaving a sagging skyline between, above Coire na Creiche. On this occasion the cloud base never lifted from the east end of the ridge, and this cloud base never lifted from the east end of the ridge, and this made by far the best shape, leaving Sgurr Alasdair with no rival, and the rising diagonal of the cloud base formed an interesting balance to the diagonal direction of the loch. A gift from Heaven of which I was glad to take advantage.

The colour varied from the smoky blue-grey – cobalt and vermilion – of the Cuillin, through the shadowed moorlands of ultramarine and light red, broken here and there by pools of sunlight showing a croft or two and some small patches of cultivation, to the local colours of grass and heather of the foreground lit up by weak sunlight.

Chapter 14

Scotland

My first introduction to the highlands and islands of Scotland was in 1932, when I went with a friend, Ralph Deane, in his Alvis sports car to climb the Cuillin ridge of Skye. We camped in our flimsy tent on some grassland close to the village of Carbost because, with a car, this was strategically placed for reaching either end of the ridge or any peaks between.

Starting with the four pinnacles of Sgurr nan Gillean, we climbed fairly modest sections of the ridge in showery weather – for it was late July – descending only once to the magic encircled water of Loch Coruisk, and spending most of the time on Sron na Ciche, above Loch Coire Lagan, and on the Cioch. The rough gabbro was a delight to the feet, making possible the ascent of gradients quite impossible on the smoother rocks of Lakeland.

On the last two days of our fortnight the rain came down in steady torrents, and everything we had became a soggy mess. I had noticed a new bungalow in the village with the name Wilmar on the gate and the magic words, 'Bed and Breakfast', so we decided to treat ourselves to dry beds and real cooking. It was my first meeting with the Steele family. Father William ran the post office and general store while mother Mary presided over their new home, two of the sons farmed and the youngest John was training to be a schoolmaster. The one daughter, Peggy, cooked the most exquisite and plentiful meals and generally dried us out. We happened to be their first customers in their new venture into tourism and, naturally, on our return home, we told many friends about their warm hospitality. The result was a Christmas present from the Steeles of a leg of tasty Skye mutton, and, next Christmas, a chicken.

I spent the whole of June of the following year on Skye with a fellow member of the Fell and Rock Climbing Club, J. V. T. Long, and the only rain we had was for half of one day. Not having a car, we stayed at the Sligachan Hotel for the northern end of the ridge, seeing the legendary Professor Norman Collie sitting alone and missing his friend and climbing companion, John Mackenzie, both

The Cuillin and Loch Scavaig, Skye (1936)

men from whom some of the Cuillin peaks were named, as they had made the first ascents. Then we went on to stay with the famous Mrs Chisholm in the post office at Glen Brittle. Day after day we enjoyed morning heat haze gradually thinning out into clear hot sunlight, giving us long hours of delightful traversing of acres of rough warm rock with almost dreamlike ease.

One day I set off alone carrying my painting gear, sleeping bag in its cover and plenty of Mrs Chisholm's bannocks filled with fried bacon. I reached the ridge at Sgurr Sgumain, painted all day in two directions, descending to tiny Loch Coire Grunnda towards dark for a meal beside its sandy beach, and still able to draw until eleven. When I awoke in the early hours I wondered where I was, what was the sound of wind among the rocks, and quite prepared for any strange happening, even for the appearance of Fingal and his giant deerhounds. On the following day I painted seawards, with a buttress of gabbro on the right and the dual form of the purply-grey island of Soay floating in a greeny-grey sea and the mountainous isle of Rhum, bluer, away on the horizon. I shall always treasure the timeless experience of spending two days and a night alone on the Cuillin.

Later, from Torran, beside Loch Slapin, we climbed all over the slabs and buttresses of Blaven and Clach Glas, returning sometimes around eleven at night for a meal and a welcome from Mrs Mackinnon, who was not at all put out by our lateness as her husband was out fishing until the early hours. Thirty seven years later, one of the Mackinnon boys, by that time a man of fifty, remembered not only me but also our conversation word for word. Persons are still so valued on Skye, and long may it remain so.

My next visit to Skye was in October 1934, driving an ancient bull-nosed Morris two seater with a 'dickey' seat behind, exposed to all the weather. Beside me sat my seventy-year-old mother and, in the 'dickey', my sister Una and my friend Jim Cameron. We crossed over to Skye by Mam Rattigan, Glenelg and Kylrhea, stopping at the Sligachan Hotel for a welcome glass of neat Drambuie whisky and staying for ten days with the Steeles at Carbost.

Jim and I were on the Cuillin on most days, Jim apparently ascending the three thousand or more feet with the greatest of ease, occasionally adding a few boulders to his load to increase his carrying power. One day we left the Morris, with its mock leather hood up, by the road above Glen Brittle. When we returned the hood had been stripped to its bare frame and a herd of well-satisfied Highland cattle were standing round the car. Fortunately we found a man in Portree who made us a new cover of the same material while we waited. Another day, as we were driving along a narrow road, Jim remarked, 'Look at that golden eagle!' I replied, 'No, It's a buzzard.' and so we continued until the car landed in a ditch. A green Rolls-Royce pulled up, debouching its elegant passengers and their liveried chauffeur who donned a green apron, produced a spade and tried in vain to help us. Suddenly over the hill appeared a small black Ford. A small square man leapt out, seized the front of my car, lifted it on to the road, jumped back into his own car and sped away almost before we could thank him.

It was not until 1960 that I took Ophelia to Skye, together with a young Swedish girl, Karin, who had been running our home while Ophelia completed a sculpture commission. On this occasion we travelled in the perfect kind of transport for a painter, a Dormobile motor caravan. This enabled us to stay anywhere we chose in those days. For two whole weeks the weather was anti-cyclonic, the month was June and the midges had not yet arrived. We camped by Loch Slapin, I painted from sunrise to dusk, and occasionally we plunged our sun baked bodies in the cold waters of the loch. One day we went early round to Elgol, joined a Soay motor boat along Loch Scavaig to its head, walked across the water-worn slabs of the Coruisk River, which must surely be the shortest in Britain, and the girls basked in the sun while I had an icy dip in Loch Coruisk. It was lovely to be there in those conditions but that great hollow, three thousand feet deep, to be truly in character needs to be seen under a canopy of moving cloud, though not quite so cataclysmic as in Turner's painting. Our welcome from the Steeles was almost as though we were members of their family who had been long from home.

One day we drove over to Talisker to camp for a night and to watch the waterfalls that float down from the 1100 foot cliffs, on a windy day never reaching the bottom. I drove the Dormobile down to the shore and walked back

Glen Lyon (1935)

to Talisker House, a Georgian mansion standing among well-grown trees, to call on Mr Cameron who had invited me to do so away back in 1932. The house and grounds looked rather neglected and I walked round, looking in at the windows until I came to the courtyard behind the house.

There stood a little thin old lady with arms akimbo and fixing me with a silent stare. I explained rather nervously what I was doing and she accepted me completely, telling me that my friend, her master Mr Cameron, had died twelve years ago and asking me to fetch my 'good lady'. I suppose it must have been half an hour before I returned with Ophelia and, in that time the housekeeper, Mary Ann Mackenzie, had composed a poem in the style of Ossian about the tall stranger who came looking round the house for his friend who now lay in his grave on dark Preshal Mor above the house. She invited us to call at ten o'clock the next morning when she showed us round the house, including the portraits of Camerons who had entertained Dr Johnson and his friend Boswell, and then we climbed up to a ledge on Preshal Mor and stood in silence round the grave enclosed in iron railings.

At some time in the mid-fifties Ophelia and I noticed that our family doctor, Eric Fothergill, was looking rather weary and worn, so I took him to Sutherland in my 1936 Armstrong-Siddeley 18 horse power convertible car, together with two tents. As we pitched these above Kylesku ferry a wind was rising and there was rain in it, for it was in August. Much later I woke in pitch darkness to find that my tent had blown away in the 70 mile an hour gale, so I gathered all my belongings and gradually transferred them through the almost horizontal rain into my capacious car. This was rocking so violently that sleep was impossible, so I cooked and ate a plate of porridge and settled down to write an article for the Fell and Rock Club Journal on, of all subjects, 'Weather'. So engrossed was I that Eric's gesticulating face at the window gave me quite a shock. He was both furious with me and alarmed when he discovered, after much shouting, that both I and the tent had disappeared.

I phoned to Ophelia to send another tent, and, in the meanwhile, we stayed in

Loch Clair and Liathach (1966)

the house of John Mains, the schoolmaster of Stoer who was away for a few days. It rained most of every day for a fortnight. Between downpours I would race around choosing likely subjects for painting and, during the longer intervals, would paint.

Eric fished the whole of each day in many of the hundreds of lochans but never caught a single trout. However, the change and rest did him a lot of good, and we even enjoyed joining in a spontaneous ceilidh, or sing-song, in a farmhouse full of young people.

A few years later, after the convertible had died, and we owned an ancient Dormobile, we took an elderly friend, Mrs Vera Leigh-Hunt, to Sutherland, Vera was writing and illustrating a book on all the wild flowers of Britain so, while she and Ophelia ranged around finding many flowers strange to them, I painted along that wonderful seaboard of mid-Sutherland, revelling in such bays as Achmelvich with their white shell beaches and every variation of colour from palest turquoise to ultramarine in the water. Inland stood the strange tall peaks of Suilven, Stac Polly and their neighbours, and some of these I climbed and painted, with foregrounds of moorland, lochans or white shell beaches.

Apart from short visits I did not go to Scotland to paint until May of 1982, immediately after a heavy fall of spring snow. Having stayed the first night at Bridge of Orchy, I was able to paint Buchaille Etive Mhor in the morning sun, its rock faces surrounded by a network of snow, cobalt blue in the shadows of crack and gully. I went on to stay for a week in Glen Spean with some forty friends in the Fell and Rock Climbing Club, the good weather, sun with plenty of interesting clouds, holding for the following three weeks. While my younger friends spent their days and energy amid the snows of the high peaks, I painted every day from lower levels such as Ben Nevis from Gairlochy, Ben Alder from Pattack Moor and Craig Meagaidh from the sandy foot of Loch Laggan, showing a glimpse of the great rock face of Coire Ardur, some two and a half miles across and 1700 feet in height.

I had been fortunate enough in 1934 to be in the party – H. M. Kelly, J. H. B.

Buchaille Etive Mhor (1982)

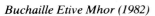

Lancet Peak, Ben Alder (1934)

Bell, R. W. Allan and myself – that climbed the first ascent of the first route, Staghorn Gully, that had ever been made on the crag.

I went on alone to stay for two weeks on Skye, starting at Ardvasar on the point of Sleat. From its western shores I painted the mountains around the outlets to the sea of Loch Hourn and Loch Nevis, while, from the western shores, the distant Cuillin made a fretted skyline beyond the nearer headlands around Tarskavaig – a truly Norse name – and Ord. One day I spent on the moor above Loch Slapin awaiting the final rising of great plumes of cloud from Blaven and Clach Glas, and, the next day, from Elgol – a place drenched with light from sky and sea – I was able to paint the island of Rhum some fifteen miles away on the horizon on a morning clear enough to show the cloud shadows and the peak of Ben Mor. On a clear golden evening the whole of the Cuillin ridge stood against the sky, blue shadows dividing the golden peaks and, eventually, the sun setting behind Garsbheann and flinging a pathway of golden light across Loch Scavaig.

It was almost a homecoming to arrive at Carbost and to meet all the remaining Steele family down to the third generation, Bill, running the same post office store that his grandfather, William, ran when I first met them fifty years ago. I stayed with the Ruardh Steeles in great comfort and, as the clouds fell lower each day on the Cuillin, my visit became more of a social one, due to the warm hospitality of the Cuthbert Wakefields of Drynoch Lodge. One Sunday afternoon I called at Orbost House, where David and Marion Roberts have a picture gallery attached to their interesting Georgian house. It was good to meet them, to see their paintings and also work by my friends Bernard Eyre Walker and Jill Aldersley.

I drove 377 rainy miles home in one day, and it was good to be able to look forward to my next tour of Skye and Sutherland in October, when the siennas of moorland and blue-blacks of mountains are magnificent and there are no midges. When I am in that part of Scotland I wonder why I ever want to go and paint anywhere else for, to my mind, it is the most colourful country in the world in autumn, winter and spring, and the mountains are so dramatically mingled with the sea and the inland waters.

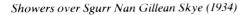

Showers over Sgurr Nan Gillean Skye (1934)

NORDFJORD AND HORNELEN, NORWAY (1968)

My wife and I had spent the October night in our old motor caravan beside a small lake, Movatnet, and descended in the early morning to the fishing village of Maurstad, near the outlet of Nordfjord to the sea.

The morning sun shone through crystal clear air – as clear as I have ever seen in Norway – Illuminating every object, from the worn boulders, draped with golden seaweed, to the ancient wooden boathouses with nets hanging outside, to the fishing boats at their moorings, on to the rocky headlands and islands, away out to the distinctive profile of Hornelen, ten miles away, with its great cliff face that falls over a sheer 2000 vertical feet to the sea.

While Ophelia was making close-up studies of decorative drapes of hanging nets, I painted all I could see in full colour and tone, direct on to the paper without any second washes, starting with the sky, sea and Hornelen, its shadows in cobalt and crimson, and the neighbouring islands, then the colourful buildings, with crisp purple shadows of ultramarine and vermilion, right up to the foreground boulders, burnt sienna added to the ultramarine to help the aerial perspective. I completed the painting in about three hours and never touched it again. That doesn't often happen.

When Ophelia joined me for our sandwich lunch, a middle-aged man, who had been watching me paint, spoke to us, in perfect English, of course, inviting us to go with him in his motor boat to see Hornelen. He was one of the heroes of the famous 'Shetland Ferry' during the second world war, and had received from his government a good pension and a splendid sea-going motor boat.

Chapter 15

Europe

Night Fishers, Cassis, Provence (1925)

Over the next few years, our next generation branched out into marriage – all four of them – so they evidently approved of the institution.

Our eldest daughter, Otalia, at the age of nineteen, married Peter Johnson, the head of the chemistry staff at Heversham School, which our sons attended; at the age of twenty John married Lesley Rushton, a girl from Oldham whom he met when he was working in London. In 1972, at the age of twenty five, Julian married Linda Ryle, who came from Newcastle, whom he had met while both were gaining degrees at Goldsmiths College of Art, London; Linda, besides having a degree and Art Teachers' Diploma, is a gifted designer and craftsman, particularly in leather. And in 1972, at the age of twenty three, Clare married Das Martin, an Indian student whom she met when they were both working for social workers' diplomas in Aberdeen.

During the eleven years for which I was president of the Lake Artists Society – a thriving art society founded in 1904 – I arranged for music recitals to be held during the summer exhibition in the large well-appointed village hall in Grasmere. Besides booking the Keswick sister and brother, Carolyn Sparey (who now plays the viola in the Scottish Chamber Orchestra) and her brother, Jonathan, (who plays the violin in the Fitzwilliam Quartet), we were fortunate enough to engage some of their young friends before they became famous and expensive, such as Moray Welsh, the cellist, Christian Blackshaw, the pianist, and our friend David Van Asch, who led the brilliant vocal group known internationally as The Scholars, for all had been trained by Sir David Willcocks and had obtained music degrees at King's College, Cambridge. It was very pleasant for us to have these young people singing in my studio and around our home.

Besides the Lake Artists Society, which kindly elected me an honorary life member, the only other art society to which I was elected is the Royal Institute

Temple of Aphaia, Aegina, Greece. (1977)

Tulli. (1983)

of Painters in Watercolours, chiefly through the effort of my old friend, Rowland Hilder.

As our young people were now living their own lives, with many visits home at holiday times, especially at Christmas, Ophelia and I took our holidays together without them. Always these included painting, especially the voyages up the west coast of Scotland, to Skye and to Norway, where we stayed with relatives for part of the time, the rest being spent touring around the mountains and fjords, sleeping and eating in our Bedford Dormobile, the ideal answer to the needs of a landscape painter who likes to paint from dawn onwards, and in places where there is no habitation. One of the parts of Norway we enjoyed especially was the high plateau of the Jotunheim, dotted with small snow-bound rocky tarns and with a skyline of the Smörstabbtinder peaks protruding from a glacier, and the masses of Fanaraaken, Glittertind and Galdhöpiggen, the highest mountains in Norway, as well as the gabbro pinnacles of the Skagastolstinder.

We usually went to Norway in June, when the days were long and the weather generally fine, or in the autumn, when the flame-like mountain birches glowed against the blue-black mountains, even in cloudy weather. Switzerland drew us for many years, when we toured with tents and all our gear in an ancient Armstrong-Siddeley open touring car of large dimensions. Part of the journey was painting and exploring, while always we spent much of our time at Mountain House, Caux.

One of the most enjoyable tours we made was to Italy, with the express purpose of seeing all the paintings by Piero della Francesca and Giotto that we could see in three weeks. First we stayed for a few days in Rome, going around with our son Julian who had won a prize at Goldsmiths College of Art to enable him to spend a year in the British School in Rome. Then on to Assisi, where we spent many hours in the upper and lower churches of the cathedral of San Francesco with the Giottos, visiting the church of San Damiano where St Clare had her nunnery and tended St Francis when he was dying; and the tiny church down in the valley, enclosed within a large edifice which overpowers it. We walked up Monte Subasio, past the monastery whose abbot helped St Francis throughout his life; and I painted the city from high up by the Rocca Minore, looking down on the city walls and the remains of a Roman theatre.

From Assisi we went on to stay in Arezzo. Much of our time we spent in the church of San Francesco, absorbing the magic and mystery of Piero della Francesca's murals, that depict the story of the finding of the true cross. This story had given the painter opportunities of great richness in illustrating the glory of the Queen of Sheba, and of the armies of the Emperor Maximilian.

It was in April, the Tuscan and Umbrian hills were clothed in delicate greens, and the red-gold of the poplars, with wild flowers emerging in the woodlands. We took the public bus for the fifteen miles to Borgo san Sepolcro, where Piero was born over four hundred years ago. He had lived much of his life in his native town, becoming eventually a member of its governing council.

Alone on the white wall of the council chamber is a mural painting of the Resurrection by Piero. In the light before dawn Christ is stepping from the tomb and looking straight out of the picture with a grave, challenging and yet loving gaze. The soldiers sleep in front of the tomb, and the dawn lights up the sky, seen through groves of oaks, which still grow on the hillside above the town. This is one of the greatest paintings in the world, and it came within a hairsbreadth of being destroyed during the war of 1939 – 1945, when the British were driving the German army northwards.

From Borgo we walked a few miles to a village built around a pointed hill, Monterchi. Close to the village and among fields and vineyards there is a cemetery with a tiny chapel. We had to find a peasant in a nearby cottage to open up the chapel. Inside, covering the back wall, is a painting by Piero. It is of a pregnant Virgin, standing under a sort of embroidered tent, the side flaps of which are held back by two angels. The virgin is clothed in a quiet blue cloak and her face has an expression of wonder and joy.

Then we had a few windy, cold days in Florence. We explored the buildings, churches and the Uffizi gallery, and the church of San Marco thoroughly, enjoying especially the Pazzi chapel, but most of the galleries were closed owing to a strike of public servants.

Haystacks, Monterchi, Italy. (1968)

After a few days in Siena, enjoying the medieval walled city and the wonderful paintings by Duccio and Simone Martine in the town hall, we went on to stay with friends near Carrara. They took us to explore Lucca, and some of the ridges and villages of the Appenines, where I did some painting on a hazy spring day, the mountains looking very high and far away.

Life was very good for us, with our young people and our seven grandchildren close by, except for Clare and her Das, who lived in Essex but came to stay at least once a year. Our family gathered especially at Christmas time, holding our dinner for the family on Christmas Eve, followed by the family service by candle light for the blessing of the crib in Grasmere's ancient church.

DAWN, LAKE OF BRIENZ, SWITZERLAND (1952)

My wife, Ophelia, and I had driven in our large 1936 Armstrong Siddeley open touring car from England, and were on our way eventually to paint and climb from Zermatt. Having spent much of a day with friends in Berne, we drove to a camp site on flat grass right on the edge of the water at the head of the Lake of Brienz. It was August, and a fine spell of weather had set in, so I woke early before dawn and set up my easel on the flat sands by the lake. This particular morning remains in my memory as the expression of perfect peace in a most lovely place. Across the lake the limestone mountain, a spur of the Faulhorn, caught the full golden light of sunrise, each buttress casting its milky-blue shadow, and the whole reflected in the almost still water, with just enough movement to fret the edges of each reflection. Across these, in horizontal spears of warm grey, cut the sandy spits in the foreground.

But the real subject of the painting was the light.

I started the painting with a large brush full of cobalt mixed with aureolin yellow right at the top of the paper, gradually adding more yellow and decreasing the blue until the lower sky was the palest of yellow greens. While this was still wet I ran in the pinks and violets of the distant mountains in varying degrees of cobalt and crimson, all the time keeping everything in a very high key.

It is a strange thing that the sun seems to rise more rapidly as soon as one begins to paint. I suppose that the effect I have painted here actually lasted for only a few minutes, but, with a trained visual memory, I was able to continue to paint this chosen moment for over an hour, long after the whole thing had changed from the magic of dawn into just the beginning of another fine day.

Chapter 16

Conference

Each year at Caux, high above the Lake of Geneva, were held conferences that brought together hundreds of people from all over the world who committed themselves to build the world much more as the Creator intended it should be.

The great building had been a luxury hotel in the 1920s to 1930s, but, during the second world war, it was used as a centre for the many soldiers who had escaped from German or Italian prison camps and sought refuge in Switzerland.

I went to Mountain House, Caux, first in 1947 to help clean up the building ready for a conference that year, and I have never worked so hard in my life. At the conference were 1200 people from many parts of the world.

One dramatic moment stays in my memory; I was sitting during a meeting behind Mme Iréne Laure, who was Secretary General of the Socialist Women of France. I knew that her son had been tortured by the nazis in a vain effort to extract the names of his friends in the 'maquis', as the French underground resistance was known. She was bitterly anti-German.

Four German men, among several Germans at Caux, stood on the platform and introduced themselves. They were the first Germans to be invited to a European conference since the war.

I saw Mme Laure's shoulders stiffen and she began to rise, but sat down again. One of the Germans was saying that he and his compatriots had been invited to Caux, and that first they wanted to apologise to all parents, especially to the French, for the harm they had done to them and their families during the war.

As soon as they had spoken I saw Mme Laure rise and make her way onto the platform. There she told us what had happened to her family and friends, and about her hatred of all Germans. She had listened to the Germans and wanted to tell them how deeply sorry she was for her hatred, and she wished to shake them by the hand.

This was the beginning of many years she spent travelling over Germany doing all she could to help heal old wounds and to rebuild their country. The German Chancellor, Konrad Adenauer, who engineered with M. Robert Schuman, the French Foreign Minister, the Franco-German Pact, said that Iréne Laure had done more than any single human being to mend relationships between the two countries.

Through the very nature of his work, the artist must spend a great deal of his time, and make many of his decisions, alone. While he is painting, the whole of himself must be concentrated upon what he is making, so that everything that he wants to say gets through. One of the most valuable lessons I learned at the M.R.A. conferences was to care for others, and to work with them towards a common purpose. It was a very difficult lesson for me and it often caused me great pain and frustration, but I realised how much farther I had to go in order to become a loving person. The actual 'how' for me was to wake up much earlier than before, read a passage in the bible – the most helpful being the teaching and life of Jesus – think it through on the level of where to start now, by the absolute standards of Christ, and decide to give all that I knew of myself to all I knew of God.

The teaching of Christ in practical terms was well expressed by Peter Howard at one of the conferences. 'Absolute moral standards are a guide in life. They are like the north star. For centuries mariners have steered by the north star. It is a fixed point in the sky. It is yet to be recorded that any ship has reached the north star, but it is true that, on every ocean, mariners discern from that star where their position is and where they need to head. And absolute moral standards, for those who lack faith, may be a good starting point if they wish to play their part with all of us in a revolution that will change this country and the world.'

I found it was necessary and natural to share my findings with another person whom I trusted and who was also living in this way, and also sometimes to someone they might help. This, of course, included my family and those with whom I worked. One unexpected result of becoming a more caring person showed in my painting. Because of this new quality in my life, what I had to say in painting and writing was understood and accepted by most people, and this left me free to give all of myself to the work in hand.

It was during these conferences that I began to realise that they were a sort of pilot light to nothing less than a step forward in evolution for the whole of humanity.

Sometimes I tended to become rather unreal in this new dimension of

Mme Iréne Laure (1982)

Dr. Buchman and M. Robert Schuman at Caux (1948)

Caux and Montreux (1948)

thinking. I recall, on one such occasion, going to visit Frank Buchman who had been unwell and was resting in bed. I began to tell him of some of the things I had been trying to learn. He waited patiently until I had dried up, and said: 'Heaton, tell me more about those four children of yours who wear out the seats of their pants sliding down the rocks.'

Such encounters and decisions and new beginnings, on personal, racial and national scales, have been happening from then to this day at Caux, the European Headquarters of Moral Re-armament. As well as Caux there are centres in many countries – India, Japan, Australia, France, Germany, Ireland, America and many others.

The two main centres in Britain are the Westminster Theatre, Palace, Street, London, and, in the North, Tirley Garth, Tarporley, Cheshire. The theatre is a centre for all the arts, holding occasional exhibitions of paintings, but working mainly through the art of the theatre. Throughout the year, plays and musicals that answer the problems of our age are constantly being produced, each of a highly professional standard, sometimes including in the cast those who work full time in M.R.A. for no salary, and at others well-known and highly gifted professionals. Each day during term a number of schools send their pupils for a day behind the scenes of a London theatre. The morning is spent exploring all the technical arrangements and meeting the staff. After a meal, a full scale production takes place on the stage. Then, in the evening, the current production is held for the general public.

In July 1981, I had the pleasant duty of opening at the Westminster Theatre an exhibition of watercolours by Ronald Mann, playwright and theatre director, who, since he returned to England, having escaped from an Italian prison camp minus one eye, had become increasingly interested in painting on the Lakeland Fells. He used to go out with Bernard Eyre-Walker and me on painting expeditions, usually in spring and autumn, and developed his own style of interpreting the changing lights among the fells, usually painting from high levels. He exhibited many of his watercolours painted in that very spring, and they were highly appreciated and sold well. As always, he gave all the proceeds to further the work of the theatre. Incidentally, it was Ronald Mann, who, more than any of my friends, urged me to write this book.

At Tirley Garth, a mansion standing on an elevated ridge in the Cheshire countryside not far from the industrial cities of the North, there are people coming and going from many parts of the world, exchanging views and making new decisions for themselves, their nation and the world. Often conferences between opposing sides, such as employees and employers, are held here, resulting in important, though not publicised, decisions. All the work of M.R.A. is voluntary, in each country. I have today been speaking to a busy housewife who, over the last few years has made 14,000lbs of marmalade to sell in aid of Asia Plateau, the M.R.A. centre of India, 160 miles from Bombay.

Dent Du Midi from Caux (1948)

Besides these centres are thousands of homes throughout the world, including our own, where people meet to find out together how to build the world as God intended it to be, without barriers of class, colour or creed. We find that the best way to heal a wrong in the world very often is to start with oneself and the next person.

At the present moment in our history the greatest concern of millions of people is over the question of nuclear armament. I am as concerned as anyone that a nuclear war should not happen. Anyone in their right senses must be so. But I doubt very much that unilateral disarmament by itself will avoid such a war. We need, at the same time as disarming, to change the hearts and minds of millions of ordinary people, including statesmen, in every country in the world. This may seem to most of us an impossible aim, but to have a partial or lesser aim is to end finally in disaster.

What gives me hope in face of such a challenge is the success that M.R.A. is having among people of such differing creeds, and those also with no creeds at all but only ideologies that hold within themselves the seeds of their own destruction. A network across the world of people living lives guided by God is really, for me, the only practical aim for the future of mankind, and I am immensely grateful to be taking part in it.

DOWN THE CUMBRIAN ESK (1956)

The Cumbrian Esk and its tributary, Lingcove Beck, together with Langstrath Beck in Borrowdale, are the wildest, rockiest, most colourful and interesting mountain streams in England.

Veins of pink granite have intruded into the blue-green Borrowdale volcanic rock at intervals down the valley, and the water is crystal clear. So, even in the bed of the stream, one can see rounded stones and boulders of green slate lying among the ribs of granite, smoothed and rounded by the force of the fast-flowing river. The interesting problem for the painter was to show the slightly warm-green reflection of the rocks on the right, becoming increasingly blue to the left where it reflected the sky, and yet to show the bed of the stream gradually diminishing into blue. The only way to paint this was by spending some time first in close observation, and then translate this complex scene into as simple a statement as possible, taking great care with tone values, sometimes extremely subtle, as well as the symphonies of light and of local colour.

It was painted in May, when the bracken was still a washed-out red, the grasses ochre to green and the hawthorns and birches were at their loveliest.

This was just above the junction with Cowcove Beck. For several miles upstream are the most delightful waterfalls and rapids tumbling into deep clear pools, delightful to plunge into on a hot day.

From childhood onwards the human animal needs a certain amount of water play and I have never outgrown my delight of playing around in a mountain stream and lying stretched out on smooth water-worn rocks to dry in the sun.

Chapter 17

Ophelia

As each of our children grew into the age when they began thinking for themselves they were full of questions and, of course, it was nearly always their mother whom they asked. One day, when Ophelia was weeding peas in the garden while little John watched, he suddenly asked 'Where is God, momma?' Ophelia told him that God was everywhere. 'Is He in the house? Is He in the air? Is He in the ground?' Then, 'I know where God is, He's in the ground, pushing up the peas.'

Soon after this Ophelia produced one of her all-too-rare paintings. It was tall and narrow. At the base was a mound of earth in which could be seen rocks, stones, roots and insects. To each side were distant views, one of mountains, the other of seas, and above was flying a skein of wild geese in V formation. All these spoke of things of the earth which she loved so strongly. Out of the centre of the earth and well rooted in it was a plant that grew tall and straight against the sky, which was golden below, with distant columns of showers. Then came storm clouds, dark, blue-black, from which flashed tongues of lightning. All these illustrated the gleams and storm of childhood and youth. Then, above them, were the tops of great white cumulus clouds sailing across skies of palest turquoise that, higher up, became a warm cobalt blue, and, through it, curved high cirrus clouds of feathery white. This denoted our emergence into the calmer ages of our lives, and the cirrus clouds led upwards. Against all this grew the tall plant with close-fitting leaves, and, at its head, a beautiful white flower with star-like petals and a golden calyx, shaped rather like a crown with its stamen pointing to heaven.

We always called it 'The Flower of Understanding'. It hung for years above the fireplace in our living room, and became the starting point of many deep conversations and friendships. In 1975 we hung it in the gallery so that more people could see it. I wrote a poem about it, which a great friend of Ophelia's, Joan Tebbutt, inscribed in lovely script. It went:–

The Flower of Understanding (1955)

> *Our Genesis is in the earth*
> *(see the rocks, roots and creatures).*
> *We experience earthly delights*
> *in sea, mountains and the flight of birds.*
> *We grow through the storms of childhood,*
> *youth, adolescence, maturity:*
> *more calmly emotionally, perhaps,*
> *as we learn wisdom.*
>
> *If we continue to grow straight*
> *towards what light we can see*
> *we shall partake of the light.*
> *And the Source of all Light*
> *will make of us something*
> *of beauty and character.*
>
> *This can be the revelation*
> *for which we are created.*

At the request of a friend, Ophelia had written down some of her general thoughts on art, which follow.

Thoughts on Art

"Art at its best is a communication from the Creator through man to man.

It is also a communication from man to man.

At its lowest it is only a communication from self to self, and, as such, sterile except to a few like-feeling persons who can respond.

The artist's job is to bring back into mundane material living the eternal, the infinite, the spiritual and make the intangible tangible. 'And the Word became flesh'.

Art is a language that is universally understood in time and space. It can by-pass the reason and speak direct to the emotions, so it is very powerful.

As it is a language in itself, it is sometimes impossible to translate or explain works of art. We learn the language as we need it.

Challenge (1969)

In mediaeval times art and craft were not separated as they are now. The artist was also the architect, engineer, sculptor and craftsman.

A work of art must be honest, sincere, first hand experience, or the expression of desire for first-hand experience. It does not have to be beautiful in the sense of being pleasing to all. Some tortured, ugly, groping and apparently negative works or art, if they spring from actual experience and are not using the ugliness to attract to the artist's self, can be great.

If he is honest and in real touch with people, the artist cannot help expressing the age he lives in. To try to go back to the past produces second-hand horrors.

The age we live in needs artists with vision as prophets of the future. Their vision may be dark or light. Both can serve by making the positive and negative trends of their age tangible enough to arouse others' apathy and automatic reactions and become adult, with free wills to use in a freely chosen direction.

The art of a nation does affect as well as reflect its age. The designs of contemporary artists, though at first laughed at, are usually accepted and absorbed into the design of living as a whole, for better or for worse.

Art should not become an alternative to creativeness in all other fields, as it did in the decadence of late Greece and Rome. Art must be the spurs, the seeking, the signposts, the signs, the growing bud of the evolution of Man.

Artists and craftsmen need to use the materials, tools and resources of the age they live in. The speed, accuracy and effortlessness of modern tools. Yet they need to retain the inner harmony of a state of 'unresting, unhasting and silent as light', and trust in eternal values.

The eternal must in all ages penetrate and be set free through the material, actual, factual, earthy incarnations of today.

'The Word was made flesh' must at all times be happening, or there will be no vitality to carry a people over the self-destructive forces within and without.

Modern art is perhaps only truly understood by those who try and strive to express something greater than themselves in some tangible form and in their own languages.

The speed of mass production and of building and the discovery of new techniques all have their influences on the production of the artist. He has to learn to live in the world with the problems of speed, of mechanisation, of the overtime pay packets, the competitive ideological battle for power, and materialism at large in a way that has perhaps never been so universal.

The crudities of modern art are sometimes honest, and express the crude untrained character of this evolutionary or decadent age we live in. Whether it is evolutionary or decadent is probably as yet unknown. It may still be in our power to choose. Can art help this choice? Should it? Does it? How can it? Who will? Does art follow or lead the morality of a people? Is it for a few or for all? Does it express the depths of a people, or only the depths of an artist?

Stone speaks less of the artist than does bronze, of his feelings, his transient physical touch. It speaks more slowly, colder, quieter, more impersonal and out of time, less human and more elemental.

Very often the artist can express in his work the apparent contradiction of his character. Only by knowing Hell can he desire Heaven enough to create an image of it. By humility and a sense of lonely impotence, he can be used as a tool of power and purpose if he will strive towards the deepest longings in his heart and the highest vision of his mind.

Creative energy is the greatest power on earth. It is the divine and the natural gift of God to all living things human and non-human. To the human is also given the free will to surrender it back to the service of the Creator and so complete the full circle of His design for creative living.

The creative energy within us is aroused by many influences. It can be used by God on all the levels of creation – sex, love, work, sacrifice, art and thought and prayer – and it has the power of its source when it is controlled by its source".

During January 1975 Ophelia's right leg started to drag when she walked. Her doctor advised consulting a specialist at once, who diagnosed cancer of the brain. He and another highly qualified specialist in brain cancer advised an immediate operation. A piece of the left side of her skull was removed, and it was found that the cancer was so deep-rooted that an operation for its removal was impossible.

Madonna and Child (1973)

Ophelia. (1967)

Except for about an hour, she was mercifully in no physical pain, but for five weary months she lingered on, first in Kendal hospital and then at home, becoming more helpless day by day. She struggled hard to help herself, to move, to speak, to write and draw, but steadily became more helpless.

She died peaceful at 6 o'clock on the afternoon of August 12th 1975.

The headstone above her grave in Grasmere's cemetry is of Lakeland green slate, a stone in which she enjoyed working. At the top of the stone the sculptor, Brian Johnston, carved in low relief the head of the Flower of Understanding. Below this her name, 'sculptor', and her dates, 1915 – 1975. Below this again is carved: 'Seek ye first the kingdom of God'.

In the summer of 1973 Ophelia had modelled a Virgin and Child for the chapel of the Anglican convent of St Denys at Warminster. The Mother is a strong mid-eastern woman, full of authority, and the Child is standing on her knees, while she holds His arms apart. Both are looking slightly leftwards towards the altar and both are filled with joy. In 1975 we had another of these cast in stone mixed with fibreglass to make an extremely durable material. This is now placed on the wide central pillar of St Oswald's church in Grasmere. There is no inscription below it, but in the guide booklet is written a paragraph to explain in whose memory it is.

The last sculpture she carried out, in 1974, was one of St Francis, kneeling with arms outstretched to receive the stigmata, and through the centre of his body is a cross-shaped hole through which the light shines. This was purchased by a Catholic friend, Paul Manzi Fé, who has left it in his will to the Abbot Hall Art Gallery in Kendal.

QUIET PASTURES (1968)

In many of the years of our life together, my wife and I, and often our children, stayed at the place that was nearer our hearts than any other in the world, the hamlet of Loweswater, among the rounded fields and fellsides of Skiddaw slate at the foot of Crummock Water. We would often be lent a seventeenth century cottage across the farmyard of Low Park, where our friends, the Alexander family lived.

On our arrival, the first thing Ophelia and I would do was to walk down through the fields and hawthorns to the Pele shore, a curved bay of palest warm-grey shingle. On this evening in May, as we sat by the bay, the spirit of deep peace and joy gradually stole over our whole beings.

I made a small sketch at the time, but it was some weeks later, in recollection, that I painted a large watercolour of it.

The curtain of the dark slopes of Melbreak, painted in ultramarine and light red, seemed to intensify the golden evening light that glanced down the rounded slope, ridged with sheep trods and dotted with grazing sheep, that cast long shadows below them. These I painted in purest golden green of the new spring grass – aureolin with a hint of Winsor blue, using some cobalt in the shadows. The light curve of the bay was painted in the palest light red with a touch of Winsor blue.

But the climax of the scene was the two trees through which shone the golden sunlight. These were left until the end. The ash tree was almost pure aureolin yellow, the hawthorn modelled in pale warm greys made from cobalt and burnt sienna. Reflections in the bay were flooded on to wet paper, using the various colours fairly dry and working very swiftly.

This is the most peaceful picture that I have ever painted, expressing something of what I feel when listening to the music of Johann Sebastian Bach.

Chapter 18

Onwards

While I was in Bergen, alone in 1976, during the annual festival, I took my cousins, Johan and Hanna Vandeskog, to a recital of Grieg's music in his home by the lake. It was a lovely spring morning and we all sat round in the garden while Edvard Grieg's harmonies, played by violin and piano, flowed around us. On a rock I noticed about forty schoolgirls sitting in rapt attention. After the recital we three walked down to the edge of the Nordaas Lake and sat on a glaciated rock. We were enchanted when the girls came and sat around us and sang some of Grieg's lovely songs that my mother used to sing.

Some of this music kept sounding in my mind as I journeyed by bus along the side of the Sogne Fjord to its head, and then up the steep winding pass to the hotel Turtagrö. As I arrived, the owner of the hotel and his wife, Mr and Mrs Berge, arrived to open up the hotel for the season. This was the first day on which the snow ploughs had been able to carve a way through the deep snowdrifts that still lay on Sognefjell, the broad ridge of the Jotunheim that held hundreds of small lakes edged with rocks and snowdrifts. Here I had stayed in 1962 with Ophelia, Julian and Clare, in a great log cabin that served as a climbing hut and small hotel. We had walked and painted among the tarns and snowdrifts, and one day walked for three miles across, not up to, the glacier, Smörstabbre, from which rose the five rock peaks, Smörstabbtinder, so named from their likeness to a butter fork.

This time, as I was alone, I climbed up the fell behind the Turtagrö hotel and made a painting of the great gabbro peaks, the Skagastolstinder, that glowed pink in the evening sun. In the hotel were many photographs of climbers in action and in groups, and it was interesting to recognise among them H. M. Kelly, N. E. Odell and other mountaineering friends. Early the next morning I climbed up the fell again to paint the same group of peaks. It was a day of rising clouds that swirled among and above the peaks and snowdrifts. The bus that was to take me to Lom on the northern side of Sognefjell was the first bus to cross the ridge that year, and we drove through snowdrifts sixteen feet deep. I stayed a night at Lom, and the following day, caught the train to Oslo.

On the platform to meet me was my old friend, Victor Sparre, and he drove me a few miles to his log home beside the Oslo fjord. There I was welcomed by his dear wife, Aase-Marie, and his three lovely daughters, Sunnive, Veslemöy and Veronica.

Victor has achieved a very high reputation in Norway for his painting, several examples of which hang in the National Gallery in Oslo, and the Bergen Art Gallery. His reputation as a designer and maker of stained glass windows is international. His windows are in twenty Norwegian churches as well as in the Cathedral of the Arctic in Tromsö. He has just now completed the windows for a cultural centre in Tel Aviv.

Smörstabbre from Sognefjell, Norway (1962)

Victor Sparre (1982)

Evening Light, on Skagastolstinder (1976)

But he is known even more widely for his championing of the cause of the Russian dissidents. In his book, 'The Flame in the Darkness', translated into English by Alwyn and Dermot Mackay under that title, he tells of the way he became a believer through meeting Moral Re-armament in 1947, when I met him first at Caux in Switzerland: how he travelled the world with them: how he went secretly to Moscow to meet the believers in the home of the singer, Alexander Galitch: of his work through Norway to the world for the freedom of Andrei Sakharov, the Nobel Prize winning nuclear scientist, and of his friendship with, and hospitality to the writer, Alexander Solzhenitzyn.

Each day that I stayed with the Sparres, Victor took me around Oslo to the art galleries and the restaurants, and to the surrounding countryside – one day to a service in a church containing one of his windows when, after the service, he was asked by the pastor to speak to the congregation about the window and especially about the Russian dissidents.

As I write, a film for television has just been completed named 'One Word of Truth', from a sentence by Solzhenitzyn, 'One word of truth outweighs the whole world'. His books, and the impact of the Russian believers on the world is proving that, in Sparre's words, 'I believe that the re-birth of faith will come from those who have suffered most'.

I have just now heard that the film has won an award at an international festival for television films held in New York.

In March of the following year, 1977, I flew to Athens to see Greece and our friends the Harbornes. I booked in at an hotel in Glyfada, twelve miles from the city because, on the map and in the brochure, it looked as though it might be a small fishing village on the coast. However, even when flying in, I could see how much the flood of new concrete buildings was creeping for miles around the city, and even up some surrounding valleys.

Glyfada turned out to be completely suburban, with hotels all along the wide streets and the airport was only half a mile away. However, I made first for the Harbornes' pleasant house on sloping ground close to the centre of Athens. They

welcomed me warmly, and Mary took me around the city, including the wonderful Museum of Archaeology.

On the next day I explored on my own, first the Parthenon in the brilliant midday sun, which made me feel I was under a burning magnifying glass, being observed by some deity or other. I liked very much the Turkish quarter of Athens – the Plaka – with small white cottages and steep little lanes between. In one of them I had a cup of refreshing camomile tea with a young poet and a painter about the same age who were busy white-washing their tiny studio.

That evening I was invited to a music party at the Harbornes. About twenty people were there, and after an interestingly Greek meal, we sat around the studio and listened to an American composer, Jim Brown, playing Chopin and Bartok and some of his own charming compositions. Mary, who has a lovely soprano voice, sang for us. I found I had a good deal in common with an elderly Greek painter and his wife who had sung in opera. The husband kept on looking at a book of mine, and, when I told him that the illustrations had been painted in watercolour, he examined them closely, saying 'It's a trick. It's just a trick. It must be a trick.'

At the party, too, were an English painter, John Palmer and his wife Cora, who invited me to go out painting with them on the eastern slopes of Hymettus, with 'wild' Pentelic marble in the quarry foreground and the Aegean gleaming in the distance. One day I took a local bus to Sounion, where the remains of a temple stands on the far southerly headland, a welcome home to sailors from the Aegean. I was just settling down to paint when a coachload of Germans invaded the temple, shouting all together in the wind. Two of them took me by each arm while the rest lined up on each side for many, many photographs. I crept away.

Mary Harborne was determined that I should see an island, so she and Jim and I took an old steamer from Piraeus to the island of Aegina, not very far distant towards the Peloponnese.

On the next morning we walked up on to the spine of the island in the spring sunshine that revealed all sorts of spring flowers among the rocks, including cyclamen, grape hyacinth and small pink dianthus. We called at a monastery, where Mary had to don a long-skirted dress, a pile of which awaited visitors, by the door. On the summit of the ridge we found a ruin of a fine temple built in honour of the goddess Aphaia. While I painted, the others walked among the pines. In the afternoon we took a taxi to a tiny fishing village towards the west, and sat by the sea, eating octopus that were being caught on one side and fried in the little restaurant across the road.

I had not left enough time to stay at Delphi, much as I wanted to, so I booked on a coach. That was the only rainy day I had while in Greece, but I soon left the

Appenine Village, Italy (1972)

crowd behind and explored the Spring of the Oracle, the great theatre and the small circular temple. But the work of art that impressed me most was an archaic carving of a charioteer, his enigmatic smile and the body draped with a garment that fell in perfectly horizontal folds, giving the figure great dignity and poise. Between the rain showers I could see the towering crags of Parnassus behind and around us, and a gleam of the Gulf of Corinth far below. But there were neither silence nor eagles. Next time I visit Greece it will be to an island that has not yet been spoiled.

Life would have been almost unbearably lonely without Ophelia if my family had not rallied round me as they have done. Otalia, her husband Peter and their three daughters, Nicola, Hilary and Deborah live at Heversham, only 25 miles to the south, and often invite me over for a meal or for the day, and occasionally visit me in my home. John, his wife Lesley and their three children, Miles, Martin and Rebecca are only four miles away in Ambleside. John works in the studio five days a week, and his children often drop in, and they like to join in any job that is within their capabilities.

Julian and Linda have a flat in Ambleside with a studio for each of them, and they spend most of their time and energy there, Julian painting either Lake District landscapes or, more important for him, large canvasses based on studies made on their travels in France, Morocco, Egypt, the United States or Mexico.

After gaining the Dip. A.D. at Goldsmith's College School of Art, he was awarded a Boise Travelling Scholarship which gave him a year at the British School in Rome and in other countries. In 1970 he was elected member of the London Group, and a Fellowship at Virginia Centre for Creative Art, U.S.A. followed in 1981.

He has held three one-man exhibitions in London and one each in Durham University and the Laing Art Gallery, Newcastle. Between 1967 and 1983 he has had work in twelve group shows, including the Royal Academy and two exhibitions at the Serpentine Gallery in London.

Among public authorities that have purchased his work are:

Julian (1955)

Beach at Locarno (1983) by Julian Cooper

132

Calle Nicaragua (Under the Volcano) (1982)
by Julian Cooper

Inner London Education Authority.
University College, London.
Laing Art Gallery, Newcastle-on-Tyne.
Bolton Art Gallery, Lancashire.
Lancaster University.
Abbott Hall Art Gallery, Kendal.
Northern Arts Collection.
Arts Council Collection.
Reuters, London.

An art critic, writing on his recent work that has been inspired by Malcolm Lowry's book, 'Under the Volcano', suggests that Julian is 'concerned with the unity of the objective and subjective world' and with 'the inter-relationship of the visible and invisible', and 'the poetry of space'.

Having myself been intensely interested in all the phases of his development in which he has been exploring the grammar or art, I believe that, in his recent work, he has found his true direction, and that his work now shows much insight and perception, and, at the same time, is in the line of the tradition of great painting.

Linda does an occasional painting, though most of her time is spent at present in designing and painting leather objects, each one an original work of art, for which she has found an encouraging demand. Between them they also put in three days a week working in the Grasmere studio.

Clare, her husband, Das – both social workers – and their charming little son, Andrew, are the only ones who live some way off, in Essex, and they spend all their holidays with me, in which they take over the running of the house and the garden and make the holiday a relief and joy for the old grandfather.

Managing the studio with John is also Richard Hardisty, who has worked with us for 13 years. He is the son of a Grasmere farming family and has a deep love for anything to do with the Lake Country, together with great business ability, an eye for a good picture and a welcome for all who come in to the studio.

Last year Michael Sanderson, another young man from Grasmere, joined the studio team, and this year Barry Dineen, a young Grasmere man who is now married and is living in Windermere, has joined us to run a branch of our print gallery in Bowness-on-Windermere. Since then another young man, Anthony Cornforth of Ambleside has joined our team.

So I am indeed fortunate in having all these young people in the building every weekday, bringing with them much affection and friendship, and also the secure feeling that they are always there ready to help in any difficulty or venture.

Sometimes young people come to stay with me in my home. It seems to me surprising that they seem to enjoy the company of an old man of eighty, and it is a great privilege to find that my experiences of both light and darkness can sometimes be a help to them, especially if they are about to embark on the perilous but wonderful journey of marriage.

Of course, old friends nearer my own age are a great delight, as we travel back in memory over shared experiences, especially on mountains. And I often get on quite well with the very young.

One day, ten or more years ago, I received a message from our dear friend, Beth Alexander of Low Park, Loweswater, to ask if I would take her grandson, Jeremy, aged seven, out painting.

When I arrived he was raring to go, and had his school satchel packed with paper, paint box, brushes and waterpot.

We went down to the Crummock shore nearest Low Park. The wind from the west, down the lake, was distinctly cool. I painted the scene I love so much, explaining the reason for each wash as I went. Jeremy watched and listened for about half an hour, then he could not restrain his patience any longer, and started slapping on the colour swiftly and confidently, soon forgetting my existence.

After an hour or more later, in the teeth of the cold wind, I suggested that we made for home. Jeremy came to, and obediently packed up his kit, having done quite a good bold watercolour of a difficult subject.

He was silent on the way back across the fields. Then he stopped, and said: 'Mr Heaton Cooper, I think this is the best day in the whole of my life.'

Fairfield from the North East (1973)

MORNING SILVER,
CRUMMOCK WATER (1980)

Here we are at exactly the same stretch of pebbly shore as I was when I painted the watercolour illustrated on page 59 and where I am standing in the photograph on page 142. I have changed, and my painting methods have changed over the years, I hope. The material substance of the landscape except for the changing level of the lake, are the same.

It is the weather, the light and the time of year and day that are different. This was about from 8 o'clock to 10 o'clock on a morning in June. It had been raining during the night, and great cloud banks were still rolling over from the west, while between them, brilliant shafts of white sun lit up the fellsides, with the fresh greens of grasses and bracken, the light grey boulders and pebbles in the foreground, and, – the highest light in the painting, – the spears of white where the breezes ruffled the water across the lake.

THE SCAFELLS FROM NEEDLE GULLY, GABLE (1935)

After climbing one summers day with Jim Cameron, exploring a variety of routes on Napes Needle, we were crossing over Needle Ridge when I was arrested by the view of Broad Crag, Scafell Pike, Lingmell and the distant summit of Scafell, framed between the strong dark walls of the gully. The distances were swimming in heat haze beneath rolling atmospheric cloud banks, emphasising distance and sunlit space.

As usual I carried in my rucksack a small board and several sheets of R.W.S. paper, 15″ by 11″, my paintbox, brushes, an aluminium cup and a flask filled with water. To see the subject to its full advantage, I climbed a little way down from the top, so that the sunlit wall on the left and the shadowed one on the right framed just enough of the distant fell, with Piers Gill zig-zagging down the face of Lingmell.

I had to stand with one foot on each side of the gully, hold the board and paintbox in my left hand and hang the water pot on a thin spike of rock. The whole operation took not much more than half an hour.

I found the sketch on a dark day in January 1984, and began to see what I ought to have done, given more time and a more comfortable position, to express better the dramatic subject. So I pinned a thick sheet of R.W.S. 300lb Not surface paper on to my board, drew first the dark rock walls in umber crayon, moving on to each distant form in violet and blue crayons. With a large sable brush I flooded the whole sheet with a much-diluted wash of orange cadmium, to give the glow of the afternoon sunlight, then very quickly laid in the moving clouds in broad sweeps of cobalt mixed with crimson, then the far shapes, using vermilion with cobalt, and, for the nearer fellsides across the valley I added light red, yellow ochre and cobalt for the grasses and almost pure pale light red for the sunlit screes on my side of the valley.

Having kept all this fairly pale and atmospheric, the most exciting part of the operation was painting the walls of rock, full strength first time, starting with the sunlit rock on the left, with a soft-edged cast shadow. Then I painted the under-tone of shadowed rock in variations of mixtures of burnt sienna, crimson and ultramarine.

The final painting was the warm dark cracks and shadows that gave the character of Gable's splintered rock.

Chapter 19

Hope

In July 1977 I was invited to a conference of the arts at The Moral Re-armament Centre at Caux in Switzerland, 2,000 feet above Lac Leman – or the Lake of Geneva, as we call it – approached by a steep road with many hairpin bends. The great Mountain House seems to be poised at arms length from the rest of the world and, just as a painter occasionally needs to stand back from his work in order to see what to do next, so the delegates from many parts of the world can see there together what is needed to help the world conform nearer to the Creator's intention.

It was a conference within a larger conference of some 800 people. On the first morning I was asked to speak to the full assembly at the main meeting of the day. I took as my theme the power, and therewith the responsibility, of the artist in communicating his convictions directly through the emotions, and how important it is that he has his priorities right. 'Though shalt love the Lord thy God with all thy heart and mind and soul and strength, and thy neighbour as thyself.' I believe in the immense power for good of the creative imagination when the artist is released in the service of God.

During the whole conference there was held an exhibition of mural cartoons, easel paintings and lithographs by Jöel Mila, the Swedish mural painter who had worked a good deal with the great Finnish painter, Lennart Segestraale, whose impressive mural, 'The Water of Life' enhances the dining hall at Caux. Mila and I often sat together without the need for conversation as neither speaks the other's language. I am fortunate enough to possess one of his lithographs, a portion of a mural he painted in a seamens' chapel in Sweden.

In memory of Ophelia I presented to Caux one of her sculptures she called 'Man'. It is a tall narrow figure, of similar proportions to the figures in the west porch of Chartres Cathedral, but the torso is scooped out into a hollow, and a cross-shaped hole, not in straight lines but in vigorous growing curves, lets the light through. The head looks upwards and the arms and hands express their emptiness. It is cast in aluminium.

Occasionally we had a recital of the violin works of Beethoven, Bach and Shostakovitch played by Jonathan Sparey of the Fitzwilliam Quartet, and also piano works by several composers. I gave two talks, illustrated by slides, on mountain painting. After one of them a lovely young Egyptian student, Chesien Lennie – olive complexioned with clear blue eyes – came up and shyly gave me a poem she had written, inspired by a slide of an oil painting of mine of an ancient oak tree growing out of a rock beside Rydal Water. Some weeks later she called on me in Grasmere, together with several Egyptian students who were staying with various families in Britain, so I told her where to find the tree that had inspired me.

In the theatre each evening were performed plays, some of which were written and acted by delegates to the conference. I remember especially one play, produced and acted by young Germans, on the subject of the youth of Germany being determined to know the whole truth about the Nazi regime so that it could never happen again.

In 1979 the Abbot Hall Art Gallery in Kendal held an exhibition for a month of the paintings of three generations of the Cooper family. In the months ahead it was fascinating to track down paintings of many periods of work done by the three painters, sometimes resulting in the discovery of unknown or forgotten treasures. BBC Television sent Alastair MacDonald to interview Julian and myself in front of a large painting by Julian of his wife, Linda, and myself on an imaginary terrace overlooking Grasmere at twilight, with an exquisite evening sky to the west and gentle breezes on the lake below catching the golden light. The last question Alastair asked me was: 'In fifty years time which of the three artists will be remembered most?' When I pointed to Julian and said 'I think he might', I caught a look of delighted surprise on Julian's face.

In 1979 British Nuclear Fuels Ltd announced that they intended to draw water from Wastwater and Ennerdale Water for use at their plant at Sellafield on the coast. This led to the setting up of a Public Enquiry, and I was invited by the National Trust to speak on its behalf on the side of conservation.

Lord Hinton, who in 1976, had been awarded the Order of Merit, listened for 1¼ hours in the middle of a morning in his office at Electricity House on the Thames Embankment while I described the exquisite and vulnerable shores of the two lakes, and asked for his help. His reply was that, in his opinion, no water

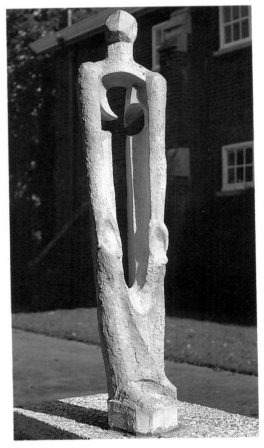

Man (1964)

October in Langedalen, Norway (1968)

should be drawn from either lake for the intended purpose, and added that no nuclear waste should ever be dumped in Cumbria.

On that same afternoon I met Lord Hunt for tea at the Royal Geographical Society and told him about the situation, for which he was grateful. Soon afterwards he joined the Friends of the Lake District and, as vice president, was asked to speak for them at the Public Enquiry.

In the event, when, at last the time came for us to speak neither of us was available, and I gather that our messages were read. The real work was done by those devoted individuals and organizations that stayed throughout the long Enquiry.

The result was a decision in our favour. Truly David and Goliath, and a great day for conservation.

During the year I usually pay at least two trips to London to see any special exhibitions of art I am interested in, to attend performances or conferences at the Westminster Theatre, or just to be with friends. The friends I almost always stay with are the three Hugh-Jones sisters who live in Finchley, just a few hundred yards from the A1 road.

Rose is the painter. She was a very special friend of Ophelia, as she is also to me. Enid is the musician, a very accomplished player of piano and organ. She was music lecturer at Whitelands Training College in London. Dorothy, the eldest, has a great gift of friendship and is a splendid cook. At 87 she plays a round of golf several times a week, and they all run their house together, and call it Heaton's second home. Usually I drive to London, as often as I have paintings or sculpture to take. Sometimes this involves driving in London, which I enjoy as a challenge, and I do not find it very difficult as I got to know my London by walking everywhere before I could afford a bus or tube.

Although I no longer climb rocks as a hobby, the climbing friends of earlier years keep up our friendship, especially the fellow members of the Fell and Rock Climbing Club, and especially at our annual general meeting and dinner meet in late October, when the rocks are still occasionally warm and trees are approaching their richest colours. In 1976 the club very kindly elected me an honorary member for my services rendered to British rock climbing.

Chris and Wendy Bonington have become our good friends since, in 1963, we were able to help find a cottage for them at Woodland, on the south western fringe of the Lake District. Chris is one of the most exceptional and competent men I have ever known, though, I have never climbed with him.

A few weeks ago I took a young friend to lunch with the Boningtons at their cottage at Caldbeck, at the northern end of the Lake District. His name is John Hawkridge, he has been crippled since birth 32 years ago, and spent half his life in a wheelchair. Since he started walking with the aid of two sticks, for his spine,

Evening Light, Rydal Water (1964)

hips and feet are twisted, he has been in a responsible job in the civil service; has climbed Scafell Pike, Snowdon and Ben Nevis alone, the latter at Easter in snow and ice; has climbed the 25 miles of Ingleborough, Whernside and Pen-y-Ghent non-stop at one mile an hour; has climbed to the foot of the rock face of the Eiger and actually climbed across rock and ice from the hole halfway up made for the railway; has visited alone thirty three countries, including Russia, and spends all his spare time working and playing with disabled people, encouraging them to 'have a go'.

John's answer to people who call him disabled is: 'Most people can't climb Everest or walk across Niagara Falls on a tightrope. Would you call them disabled?' I was quite impressed when Chris Bonington said 'Well, John you've achieved more than I've ever done.'

While I have been writing this book, Andrei Sakharov and his wife Elena, banished to live in Gorky, 250 miles from Moscow, have, by their hunger strike, gained world publicity and won the battle against the KGB to allow one of the human rights, that of freedom of movement from one country to another or within one's own country. World publicity is just what the Sakharovs and other dissidents need, and the Soviet Government fears on account of world condemnation, especially of scientists on whose aid they greatly rely.

This is a situation dangerous to evil. Again I think of Victor Sparre's words: 'The rebirth of faith will come from those who suffer most'.

It is interesting that, increasingly, the power of the Soviet Union is being confronted head-on by two great Christian leaders, both from nearby Poland, Pope John Paul II and Lech Walesa. What may happen in the future could be truly apocalyptic.

From Poland also comes news daily of cruel repression of the struggle for truth and freedom that is emerging. In the USA President Reagan is desperately striving to balance his budget, while his statesmen and generals juggle with the ethics of power. South Africa encourages raids on neighbouring independent states while, in their own country, practising hypocritical degradation of the coloured races, often in the name of Christianity and progress. The hatred and

Heaton beside Crummock Water (1983)

violence that persists in our own islands over Ireland is a disgrace to both countries, and within Britain there is bitterness, frustration and violence, especially among the young, who see no hope for the future.

Many of my friends, especially those with young families, throw themselves into working for unilateral disarmament and the banning of all nuclear power. I myself cannot see their sincerely unselfish efforts being an answer to the world's disease unless it is at the same time spreading a revolutionary change of heart and mind in all countries of the world. The only practical answer that I can see is to build a network of people across the world who are infectious believers, revolutionaries for good. This may seem impossible to those who do not see the signs of it already in existence. To expect a change in human nature may be an act of faith, but to expect a change in human society without it is an act of lunacy.

I seem to have strayed far and wide from mountain painting, yet throughout my life, now that I write it down, there seems to be a thread of continuity, linking up various strands of the pattern.

The painting of mountain country has always brought me a sense of wonder and delight intermingled with humility. I am still painting mountains and still experiencing wonder and delight and humility, though not so strongly as in my younger days and, of course, I can no longer climb so high or so fast. My adventures now are mostly journeys of the spirit and the will, and are more and more concerned with persons, learning from some and helping some along the way. I have been wonderfully helped along the way by my family and friends, who have saved me, often in spite of myself, from destruction, spiritual or physical.

Life, I find, has much of climbing and painting in it – the contemplation, the challenge, the quick decisions and the sheer joy of arriving occasionally at the place where one longed to be.

Index

Abbot Hall Art Gallery, Kendal, 71, 125, 133, 139
Achmelvich, 106
Aconcagua, 41
Aberdeen, 111
Adams, April, 36
Adams, Norman, 36
Adenauer, Konrad, 117
Aegean Sea, 111, 131
Aegina, Isle of, 112, 131
Africa, South, 142
Aiguilles Rouges, 80
Air Ministry, 63, 64, 87
Alasdair, Sgurr, 100
Alder, Ben, 106, 107
Aldersley, Jill, 107
Alexander, Beth, Jeremy, 71, 126, 134
Alexander, Ben and Margaret, 97
Alfred H. Cooper, 1
Alice Cooper, i
Allan, R. W., 107
Allinson, Adrian, Neil, 86
Alpine Club, 87
Alps, xv, 45, 80
Alston, 86
Ambleside, 13, 14, 51, 54, 61, 86, 90, 132
Amen Corner, Gimmer Crag, 43
America, 118
Andes, 42, 80
Andrew, 133
Angle Tarn, Patterdale, 79
Anglican Church, 3, 14
Anglesey, 41
Aphaia, Temple of, 112, 131
Appenines, 113, 131
Appleyard, John, 43
Archer, June, 43
Ardur Coire, 106
Ardvasar, 107
Arezzo, 112
Argentieres Pinnacles, 80
Argentina, 41, 42, 43
Arnside, 90
Arts Council, 133
Asch, David Van, 111
Asia Plateau, 118
Ash Tree Ledge, Gimmer Crag, 43
Assisi, 112
Aston, 89
Athens, 20, 130
Atkinson, Udny, 41
Atlantic, South, 41
Atomic Energy Authority, 95
'Atticus', 95
Augsburg, 4
Austin, Alan, 43
Australia, 118

BBC, 62, 139
Bach, Johann Sebastian, 126, 139
Badley, John, Laura, Mary, 85
Balestrand, i
Balholm, i
Band, The, vi
Barbizon Painters, 15
Barker, Mabel, 43
Bartok, 131
Barratt, Mrs., 14
Barrett, Michael, 56
Barrow-in-Furness, 45
Bateman, John, 71
Beckhead, 47
Bedales School, 85
Beetham Bentley, 43
Beethoven, 139
Bell, J. H. B., 43, 107

Berge Family, 129
Bergen, 129
Berne, 114
Bigland, Margot, 62
Bilibin, Alexander, 22
Billinge, Dorothea, 61, 66
Black, Adam & Charles Ltd., 7
Blacksail Hut, 45, 52
Blackshaw, Christian, 111
Blackmoor Pot, 54
Blake Rigg, Langdale, 48, 67, 79, 80
Blaven, 89, 104, 107
Blea Tarn, Langdale, 48
Blencathra, 14, 80
Blizzard Chimney, 16, 43
Boise Scholarship, 132
Bolton Town Art Gallery, i, 133
Bombay, 118
Bone, Charles, 78
Bonington, Chris & Wendy, 140
Borgo San Sepolcro, 31, 112
Borrowdale, 36, 53, 120
Boswell, 105
Boult, Sir Adrian, 62
Bowfell, vi, 54, 79, 80
Bracadale Bay, 100
Brackenclose, 62
Brandreth, 72
Brathay, River, 14, 20, 43
'Breakthrough', 97
Bridge, Alf, 43
Bridson, Admiral, xvi
Brienz, Lake of, 111, 114
Brimfell, 79
British School in Rome, 132
Brittle Glen, 104
British Nuclear Fuels, 139
Brixton, 35
Broad Crag, 136
Brown, Jim & Mary, 131
Brown Pike, 79
Brownswood, Professor, 62
Buchaille Etive Mhor, 106
Buchman, Dr. Frank, 56, 117, 118
Buenos Aires, 36, 41
Burgundy, S.S., 41
Burlington Gardens, 20, Gallery, 28
Burnthwaite Farm, 43
Burrswood, 97
Bush House, London, 64
Buttermere, 19, 66, 68, 71
Calanques, Les, 28
Caldbeck, 140
Calder Hall Power Station, 96
Calderons School, 62
'Calle Nicaragua', 133
Cam Spout, 54
Camasunary, 104
Camberley, 89
Cameron, Mr., Jim, Betty, Alastair, Hugh, 44-46,
    53, 54, 56, 104, 105, 136
Cambridge, 111
Canada, 71
Carbost, 100, 103, 104, 107
Carlisle, Bishop of, 14, 97
Carnedds, 81
Carrara, 113
Carrock Fell, 54
Carrs, 10
Cassis, 28
Casson, Sir Hugh, 64
Caudale Moor, 80
Caux, 95, 112, 117, 118, 119, 130, 139
Centipede, 45
Cézanne, Paule, 20, 27, 28, 77

Chamonix, 80
Chapel Cross Power Station, 96
Chapman, Anthony, 62
Charles, Prince, 78
Charlotte Mason College, 13, 90
Chartres Cathedral, 139
Chelsea, 20-29, 35
Chenil Studios, 35
Cheshire, 64, 118
Chester, 98
Chew, Biddy, 44
Chile, 42
Chimney Buttress, Gimmer, 43
Chisholm, Mrs., 104
China, xv, 71, 86
Chinese Painting, vi, xv, 28, 29, 79
Chopin, 131
Chorley, R. S. T., 43
Christ, 14, 31, 55, 69, 97, 112, 117
Ciche Sron na, 10
Cioch, 103
Clach Glas, 104, 107
Clair, Loch, 105
Clare, Saint, 112
Clausen, George, 23
Cockermouth, 62
Codale Tarn, 15
Coire Lagan, Loch, 103
Collie, Professor Norman, 103
Comstive, Bill & Enid, 100
Conan Doyle, Sir Arthur, 87
Coniston, Village etc., xvi, 16, 20, 45
Coniston Water, 79
Cook, Dick, 43, 46
Cooper, G. Astley, 43
Corinth, Gulf of, 132
Cornforth, Anthony, 133
Corridor Route, Scafell, 44
Coruisk, Loch, 103, 104
Courtauld, Sam, 41
Covent Garden Theatre, 51
Cowcove Beck, 120
Cowell, W. S. Ltd., 88
Creiche, Coire na, 100
Creswick Prize, 27
Crib, Blessing of the, 66, 67
Cricklewood, 51
Cross, Sid, J. M., 43
Cross Brow, 41
Crossley, Marjorie, 62
Cruachan, An, 81
Crummock Water, 58, 62, 65, 71, 126, 134, 142
Cuillin, Skye, 54, 80, 100, 103
Czechoslovakia, 64

Damiano, San. Assisi, 112
Dann, Ronald, 64
Darjeeling, 43
Das Martin, 113, 133
Davyhulme Hospital, 63
Deane, Ralph, 103
Dearden, Tom, 71
Deeley, Geoffrey, 62
Deep Gill, Scafell, 53
Deepdale, 53
Delacroix, 27
Delany, Edward, 51
Delphi, 131
Dent du Midi, 119
Derain, André, 28
Dierdre, Earle, 31
Diggle, Bishop, 14
Digre, Jacob, 8
Dineen, Barry, 133
Dodds, 80

Dôm, 80
Dorothy Kerrin Home of Healing, 97
Dorset, 96
Doughty, J. H., 43, 45
Dounreay Nuclear Power Station, 95
Dow Crags, 16, 54
Dowden, 20
Drigg, 90
Drynoch Lodge, 107
Dungeon Gill Hotel, 74
Durham University, 132

Eagle Crag, Grisedale, 53
Eagle's Nest, Gable, 27
Earle, Dennis, 27
Earnseat School, 90
Easdale, 54, 86
East Buttress, Scafell, 20
Easter Gully, 16, 43
Eden-Smith, Blanche, Waddy, 43, 52
Edinburgh, 62
Egypt, 132, 139
Eiger, 141
Elgol, 81, 104, 107
'Eliminate-A', 43
Ellide, 3
Ennerdale, 45, 52, 65, 77, 139
Ese Fjord, 1
Esk Buttress, River, vi, 19, 54, 89, 120
Eskdale, 19, 88
Essex, 113, 133
Europe, 111-113
Everest, Mount, 88
Eyre-Walker, Bernard, Dorothy, 67, 71, 107

F.A.N.Y, 63
Fairfield School, Range, 37, 79, 89, 134
Fairey Aviation Company, 31
Fan Kuan, 29
Fanaraaken, 80, 112
Fascists, British, 31
Faulhorn, 114
Faulkner, Keith, 62
Fell & Rock Climbing Club, 43, 45, 62, 74, 103, 105, 106, 140
Finchley, 140
Findelen, 80
Fine Art Society, 89
Fingal, 104
Fitzwilliam Quartet, 111, 139
Fjaerlands Fjord, 2
'Flame in the Darkness', The, 130
Fleetwith, 92, 95
Flint, Russell, 23
Florence, 62, 112
'Flower of Understanding', 123
Fothergill, Eric, 4, 105
France, 15, 35, 118, 132
Francesco, San, Assisi, Arezzo, 112
Francis, Saint, 112, 125
French Impressionists, 15
Friends of the Lake District, 140
Frithjof, 3, 13, 14, 19, 31, 55, 65

Gable, Great, 21, 35, 45, 58, 72, 80, 136
Gairlochy, 106
Galdhöpigen, 112
Galitch, Alexander, 130
Garsbheinn, 107
Gate House, Coniston, 3
Gatey, Norman, 20
Gaugin, 86
Geneva, 62, 95, 117
German Miners Delegates, 4, 8, 41, 117, 139
Germany, 118

Gillean Squrr nan, 100, 103, 107
Gimmer Crag, 43, 80
Giotto, 112
Glasgow Institute, 62
Glenelg, 104
Glittertind, 112
Glyfada, 130
Goatswater, 16, 43
God, 2, 20, 31, 54, 55, 56, 66, 71, 96, 117, 119,
    123, 139
Gogh, Vincent van, 28, 86
Goldsmiths College of Art, 22, 111, 112, 132
'Gondola', S.S., xvi
Gordon & Craig Route, 54
Gorki, 141
Gornergrat, 80, 87
Goupil Gallery, 27, 30, 35
Graithwaite, 37
Grasmere, Village, Valley, Lake, 43, 51, 56, 63, 66,
    73, 79, 82, 97
Grasmoor, 71
Gray, Lady Sophie, 41
Greece, 111, 112, 130, 132
Green, William, xvi
Greenburn, 10
Greenland, 89
Greenstone Gallery, 35
Green's Watercolour Paper, 78
Greenup Beck Gill, 38, 53
Grieg, Edvard, 129
Gresford-Jones, Bishop, 67
Grey Crags, Buttermere, 29
Grisedale, 53
Grunnda, Loch Coire, 104
Guard House, 14
Guest, Keen & Nettlefolds Ltd., 92
Guiana, British, 62

Haakon, King, 9
Hamel, Captain, xvi
Hampstead, 62
Harborne, Peter, Mary, 130
Hardisty, Richard, 98, 133
Hardknott Pass, Fell, xv, 77, 80
Hargreaves, Alan, A. T. Ruth, 43, 54
Harport, Loch, 100
Harrison Stickle, 48, 74
Harwell, 96
Hawkridge, John, 140, 141
Hawkshead, Village, Hill, 3, 71
Hawksworth, Rev. John, Desmond, Geoffrey, 14
Haws Bank, Coniston, 3
Hayes, Graham, 53
Haystacks, 79, 92
Heathwaite, Windermere, 66
Heaton Cooper, Clare, Ophelia, 85, 86, 111, 113,
    129, 133
Heaton Cooper, John Christian, 65, 86, 98, 111,
    123, 132
Heaton Cooper, Julian, Gordon, 85, 86, 11, 111,
    112, 129, 132, 133, 139
Heaton Cooper, Lesley, 111, 132
Heaton Cooper, Linda, 111, 132, 133, 139
Heaton Cooper, Martin, Das, Andrew, 111, 132
Heaton Cooper, Miles, 132
Heaton Cooper, Otalia, Valentinsen, 9, 51, 65, 111,
    132
Heaton Cooper, Rebecca, 132
Heaton Cooper, Una, 13, 36, 51, 55, 104
Hell Gill, 54
Helm Crag, 82, 90
Helvellyn, 80
Henley-on-Thames, 43, 89
Hennessy, Bill, 43
Heversham, 90, 111, 132

High Level Route, Pillar, 44, 52
High Crag, Buttermere, 58, 71
High Stile, 58, 71
Hilary, Johnson, 132
Hilder, Rowland, 112
Hill, Adrian, 36
Hillary, Sir Edmund, 89
'Hills of Lakeland', The, 56
Himalayas, 43, 92
Hinton, Lord, 95, 139
Hitchens, Ivon, 22
Holland, C. F., 43, 44
Hollow Stones, 44
Holyoake, P. W., 20
Holywath, 3, 14
Home Guard, 63, 64
Hopkinson's Crack, 44
Hornelen, 108
Hourn, Loch, 107
Howard, Peter, 117
Hsia Kuei, 28
Hugh-Jones Sisters, Rosc., 71, 140
Hui-Tsang, Emperor, 28
Hungerford Bridge, 20
Hunt, John, Joy, Sally, Prue, Susan, Jenny, 43, 53,
    88, 140
Huxtep, Dan, 30
Hymettus, Mount, 131

India, 118
Ingleborough, 141
Inner London Education Authority, 133
Intermediate Gully, 16
Ireland, 118, 142
Italy, 112, 113, 131
Ivens, Betty, 46

Jackson, Ernest, 21
Japan, 118
Jesus, 87, 117
John, Augustus, Edwin, 22
Johnson, Deborah, 132
Johnson, Doctor Peter, Brian, 86, 105, 111, 125,
    132
Jotunheim, 112, 129
Joyes, Margot, 65

Karin, Stenius, 104
Kelly, Harry M., Pat, 43, 44, 45, 51, 52, 54, 106,
    129
Kelsick Grammar School, 13
Kendal Town Schools, 20, 54, 61, 71, 90, 125, 139
Kentmere, 91
Kern Knotts Chimney, 21
Keswick, 56, 85, 111
Kidlington Airfield, 64
Kilnshaw Chimney, 78
King Henry VII Chapel, 64
King's College, Cambridge, 111
King's Road, Chelsea, 20, 35
Kipling Grove, Gimmer, 43
Kirkstile Inn, 63
Kirkstone Pass, 78
Kirkus,Colin, 43
Knott House Farm, 54
Korda Brothers, 51
Kvikne Family Hotel, i
Kylrhea, 104
Kylesku Ferry, 105

Lady Margaret Hall, Oxford, 56
Lagan, Loch Coire, 103
Laggan, Loch, 106
Laing Art Gallery, Newcastle, 132, 133
Lake Artists Society, 97, 111

145

Lake Road, Ambleside, 13, 41
'Lakeland Portraits', 88
'Lakes', The, 88
Lambourn, George, 22
Lancashire, Caving & Climbing Club/County, 1, 45
Lancaster University, 133
Langdale, Great, Little, vi, 9, 10, 19, 43, 48, 51, 54,
    55, 62, 74, 77, 79, 80, 85
Langedalen, 140
Langstrath Beck, 38, 54, 120
Lapland, 9
Laure, Mme. Irène, 117
Laverdet, Marc-Henri et, 51
Lederer, Marianne, 63
Leeds, 98
Leicester Gallery, 35
Leigh-Hunt, Vera, 106
Lennie, Chesien, 139
Levens, 71
Levers Water, 4
Lewis, Rev. Francis, 14
Liathach, 105
Ling Point Crag, 64, 65
Lingcove Beck, 99, 120
Lingmell, 136
Lingmoor, 48, 74, 77, 80
Lining Crag, 53
Lion and the Lamb, 82
Little gully, Pavey Ark, 54
Liu Hai Su, 28
Liverpool, 41, 98
Liu Hai Su, Professor
Llandudno, 45
Locarno, 132
Lom, 129
London, 7, 20-29, 46, 51, 62, 64, 89, 98, 140
London Group, 132
Long, J. V. T., 103
Longland, Jack, Ruth, 43, 44
Looking Stead, 52
Lord's Rake, Scafell, 53
Lovat's Regiment, Lord, 53
Low Park, 71, 126, 134
Lowe, George, 89
Loweswater, 63, 71, 126
Lowry, Malcolm, 133
Lucca, 113
Lucy, Sir Thomas de, 71
Lutheran, Faith, 2
Lynas Bay, 41
Lyndhurst, 87
Lyon Glen, 104

Ma Yuan, 28
McAll, Ken, Francis, Elizabeth, 86
Macdonald, Alastair, 139
McKay, Alwyn, Dermot, 130
Mackenzie, John, Mary-Ann, 103, 105
Mackinnon Family, 104
McIver, Edith, Line, 41
Madonna & Child, 97, 125
Mains, John, 106
Mam Rattigan, 104
Man, Isle of, 64, 139
Manchester, 63, 98
Mann, Ronald, George, 30, 79, 118
Manzi-Fé, Paul, 125
Marco, San, Florence, 112
Margate, 36
Mars, 19
Marseille, 28
Mathilde, Marie Valentinsen, i
Matterhorn, 80
Maud, Queen, 9
Maurstad, 108

Meagaidh Craig, 106
Melbreak, 58, 63, 64, 65, 71, 126
Mendoza, Rio, 42
Mexico, 132
Mickledore, vi, 21
Middle Row Farm, 52
Mila, Jöel, 139
Miles, Ashley, Ellen, 44
Miles, Heaton Cooper, 132
Mill Gill, Langdale, 54
Millans Park, Ambleside, 13
Millard, Pat, Canon Hall, 22, 35, 36
Mines Beck, Coniston, 9
Ming Dynasty, 28
Mischabel Range, xv
Monet, Claude, 15, 27, 77
Mont Blanc, 80
Monterchi, 112, 113
Montreux, 118
Mor, Ben, 107
Moral Re-Armament, 56, 95, 117, 118, 119, 130,
    139
Morocco, 132
Moscow, 130, 141
Moss Gill, Scafell, 53
Mountain House, Caux, 95, 112, 117, 139
Movatnet, 108
Muriel, Saleeby, 62
Murray, Athol, Olive, 87
Musgrave, Tony, 43

N.A.S.A., 87
Naddle Fell, 80
Nanda Devi, 43
Napes Needle Ridge, 45
Nash, Paul, 27
National Trust, 139
Naylor, Ella, 52
Nazaire, Saint, 53
Nazi Regime, 139
Needle Gully, Gable, 136
Newcastle, 2, 8, 98, 111
New Forest, 87
New York, 42, 130
New Zealand, 89
Nevis, Ben, Loch, 106, 107, 141
Niagara Falls, 141
Nibthwaite, xvi
Nicaragua, 133
Nicola, Johnson, 132
Nord Fjord, 108
Nordaas Lake, Bergen, 129
North Wall, Pillar, 52
North-West Climb, Pillar, 45
Northern Arts, 133
Norway, 1, 80, 108, 112, 129, 140
Oakburn School, Windermere, 62
Oaks Farm, Ambleside, 20
Odell, Professor N. E., 129
Olav, Prince, King, 9
Old Dungeon Ghyll Hotel, vi
Old Man, Coniston, xvi, 16, 79
Oldham, 111
'One Word of Truth', 130
Ophelia, 61, 86, 123-125, 129, 132
Orbost House Gallery, 107
Orchestra, Scottish Chamber, 111
Orchy, Bridge of, 106
Ord, 81, 107
Orkneys, 95
Osborne, Marjorie, 62
Oslo, 129, 130
Osmaston, Gordon, June, 16, 43, 54, 55, 88, 89
Ossian, 105
Oswald's, Saint, Church, 63

Outward Bound Schools, 88
Oxenham, John, 27
Oxford Street Group, 51, 54, 56, 64, 71

P.N.E.U., 13, 89, 90
Painting Courses, 97, 98
Pakistan, 97
Palais des Nations, Geneva, 95
Palmer, John, Cora, W. T., 7, 131
Paris, 27
Parliament Square, 64
Parnassus, Mount, 132
Parthenon, 131
Paso de los Contrabandistos, 42
Pattack Moor, 106
Patterdale, 54
Pavey Ark, 43, 54, 74
Pazzi Chapel, Florence, 112
Peloponnese, 131
Pen-y-Gent, 141
Pentelicon, 111, 131
Phelps, Peter, 95
Piccadilly, London, 20, 51
Piero della Francesca, 31, 112
Pike of Stickle, 48, 74
Pillar Rock, Mountain, 44, 45, 52, 54, 63, 92, 95
Pinnacle Club, 52
Piraeus, 131
Place Fell, 80
Plaka, Athens, 131
Plarr, Victor, 20
Plata, Rio de la, 43
Poetry Society, 20
Poland, 141
Pope John Paul II, 141
Portland, Stone, Isle of, 96
Portiengrat, 80
Portree, 104
Post Impressionists, 86
Powell, Michael, 51
Pragnell, Vera, 29-31, 36
Preshal Mor, 105
Preston, 46
Prince & Princess of Wales, 78
Professor's Chimney, Scafell, 53
Provence, 27, 28
Psalm, 104th, 55
Puente del Inca, Andes, 42

Queen Elizabeth II, Her Majesty, 96
Queen's, The College, Oxford, 14
'Quest', 71

R.A.F., 64, 65
Rake End Chimney, Pavey Ark, 43
Rannerdale Knott Farm, 58, 71, 72
Raphael, 21
Raven Crag, Ennerdale, 45
Reagan, Ronald, 141
Rébuffat, Gaston, 28
Red Pike, Buttermere, 58, 71
Red Screes, 78
Regent Street Polytechnic, 62
Rembrandt, 27
Reuters, 133
Rheims Cathedral, 77
Rhum, Isle of, 104, 107
Ridyard, Nancy, 43
Rishi Ganga Gorge, Nanda Devi, 43
Risley, 96
Roberts, David, Marion, 107
Roca Minore, Assisi, 112
Roman Occupation, Catholic Church, 4, 13, 97
Rome, 112, 132
Rosario, 43

Royal Academy Schools Exhibition, 20-23, 27, 51, 62, 64, 132
Royal College of Surgeons, 20
Royal College of Music, 62
Royal Humane Society, 20
Royal Institute, 78, 92, 112, Flying Corps, 19
Royal Scottish Academy, 62
Royal Society of British Artists, 20, 30, Sculptors, 97
Royal Oak Hotel, Ambleside, 3, Borrowdale, 44
Royal Geographical Society, 140
Rucklidge, Michael, 53
Rushbearing, Grasmere, 66
Rushton, Lesley, 111
Russia, Country Dissidents, 130, 141
Rydal, 13, 57, 66, 139, 141
Ryle, Linda, 111

Saas Almagen, 80
Saint Bede, 96, 97
Saint Bees, 14
Saint Denys, 97, 125
Saint James Church, Piccadilly, 21
Saint John's Wood Art School, 22, 62, 86
Saint Luke's Hospital, Chelsea, 36
Saint Mary's Church, Ambleside, 36, 88
Saint Oswald's Church, Grasmere, 63, 66, 125
Salvation Army, 97
Sakaniski Shio, xv
Sakharov, Andrei, 130, 141
Saleeby, Caleb, Muriel, 62, 66
Sanctuary, The Sussex, 29
Sanderson, Michael, 133
Scafell Pike, vi, 20, 21, 44, 47, 48, 53, 54, 64, 80, 99, 136
Scale Beck, 63, How, 90
Scarth Gap, 68
Scavaig, Loch, 103, 104, 107
Scholars, The, 111
Schuman, Robert, 114
Scotland, 45, 80, 86, 95, 103-107
Seathwaite, Borrowdale, 46
Segestraale, Lennart, 139
Sellafield Nuclear Power Station, 139
Serpentine Gallery, 132
Sgumain, Sgurr, 104
Shamrock, Pillar, 63
Shanghai University, 28, 87
Sharp, William, 66
'Shetland Ferry', 108
Shipton, Eric, 43, 88
Shostakovich, 139
Sickert, Walter, 23
Side Pike, Langdale, 48, 74, 77
Siena, 113
Simon's Nick, 4
Simone, Martine, 113
Sims, Charles, 20
Sinker, Paul, 44
Skagastölstinder, 80, 112, 129, 130
Skelwith Force, 14, 43
Skiddaw Slate, 58, 71
Skye, 54, 80, 89, 100, 103, 107, 112
Slab & Notch, Pillar, 45
Slapin, Loch, 104, 107
Sleat, Point of, 107
Sligachan Hotel, 103, 104
Smörstabbre, 129
Smörstabtinder, 80, 129
Snowdon, 141
Soay, 104
Sogne Fjord, Fjell, 1, 80, 129
Solheim, 3
Solzhenitzyn, Alexander, 130
Somervell, Howard, Leslie, 43

Soper, Jack, 43
Sounion, 131
Sourmilk Gill, Easdale, 54
Soviet Union, 141
Sparey, Carolyn, Jonathan, 111, 139
Sparre, Victor, Aase-Marie, 129, 130, 141
Speaker, G. R., 43
Spean, Glen, 106
Stables, Jonathan, 43
Stac, Polly, 106
Stagg, Family, 63
Staig, Ben, 80
Staghorn Gully, Coire Ardur, 107
Stallybrass, Bill, Margot, 62
Stamford Bridge Studios, 27
Steel Fell Tarn, 88
Steele Family, 103, 107
Stickle Tarn, 34
Stock Beck Ghyll, 13, 54
Stoer, 106
Strands Hotel, Wasdale, 95
Strong, Arthur, 56
'Studio' Magazine, 30, 35, 41
Sty Head, 55
Subasio, Mount, Assisi, 112
Suilven, 106
'Sunday Times', 95
Sung Dynasty, 28, 29
Sussex, 7, 22, 27, 31, 35
Sutherland, 105, 106, 107
Swinburne, 20
Swirl How, 79
Switzerland, 112, 114, 117, 130, 139

Talisker House Bay, 104
'Tarns of Lakeland', The, 88
Tarskavaig, 107
Tebbutt, Joan, 123
Tel Aviv, 129
Temple Sowerby, 53
Tensing, Norkay, 43, 88
Thames, 89, 139
Thirlmere, 22, 24
Thurso, 95
Tilman, H. W., 43
Tirley Garth, 118
Tjugum Church, 2
Tophet Bastion, Gable, 35
Torran, 104
Torver Beck Moor, 43, 79
Triftthorn, xv
Troltindener, 80
Trolstigheimen, 80
Tromsö Cathedral, 129
Trondhjem Cathedral, 8, 19
Troutbeck, 22, 61
Tryfan, 45, 52, 81
Tsung Ping, xv
Tulli, 112
Tung Pei-Yuan, 29
Turner, J. M. W., 104
Turtagrö, 80, 129

U.S.A., 87, 132, 141
Ufezzi Gallery, Florence, 112
Ullinish, 100
Ullman, James, 43
Ulverston, 8, 9, 61
University College, London, 133
Upper Eskdale, vi, 30, 54
Valentinsen, Mathilde, Otalia, Rasmus, 1
Vandeskog, Johan, Hanna, Knut, Veiga, 129
Vevey, 62
Vickery, Fred, 30
Victoire, Mont Sainte, 28, 77

Victoria and Albert Museum, 51
Vienna, 51
Viney, T. L., 95
Virginia Centre for Creative Art, 132
'Volcano, Under The', 133
Volunteer Training Corps, 19
Wakefield, Cuthbert, Elizabeth, 107
Walden, Lord Howard de., 41
Walesa, Lech, 141
Wales, Province, Prince and Princess of, 45, 78 81
Wansfell Road, 13, 20
Warminster, 125
Warne, Frederick & Co. Ltd., 56
Warnscale Crags, 68, 92
Wasdale Head, 19, 43, 52, 74, 77, 95
Wastwater, 32, 62, 65, 95, 139
Water Park, xvi
Waterlow, Joan, 22
Watson, Sir William, 41
Weisshorn, 80, 87
Wellington Square, National Gallery, 20
Welsh, Moray, 111
West, Thomas, xvi
West Indies, xvi
Westminster School of Art, Abbey, Theatre, 1, 64,
   118, 140
Wet Side Edge, 10
Wetherlam, 4, 10, 79, 85
Whernside, 141
White Bridge, Grasmere, 51
'White Horse Inn', 51
Whitelands Training College, 140
Wigton Road, Carlisle, 97
Willcocks, Sir David, 111
Wilmar, 103
Wilson Family, 85
Wimbledon, 20
Windermere, 20, 61, 62, 66, 78, 133
Windy Gap, Ennerdale, 52
Windscale, 96
Winfrith Heath, 96
Winifred Gordon Bell, 62
Winterseeds, 85 – 90
Whernside, 141
Wood, Doctor, Sir Henry and Lady, 27, 62
Wood House, Buttermere, 65
Woodland, 140
Wood-Johnson, Ernest, 43
Wordsworth, William, Dorothy, Richard, 89, 97
World War I, 19
Wrynose Pass, xv, 10, 77

Y Garn, 45, 81
Yangtse River, 28
Yeastyriggs Crag, vi
Yen Tung Ko, 28
Young Communist League, 30
Youth Hostel, Blacksail, 45

Zermatt, 114